Windows® 98
Simplified™

Covers Windows 98
Second Edition

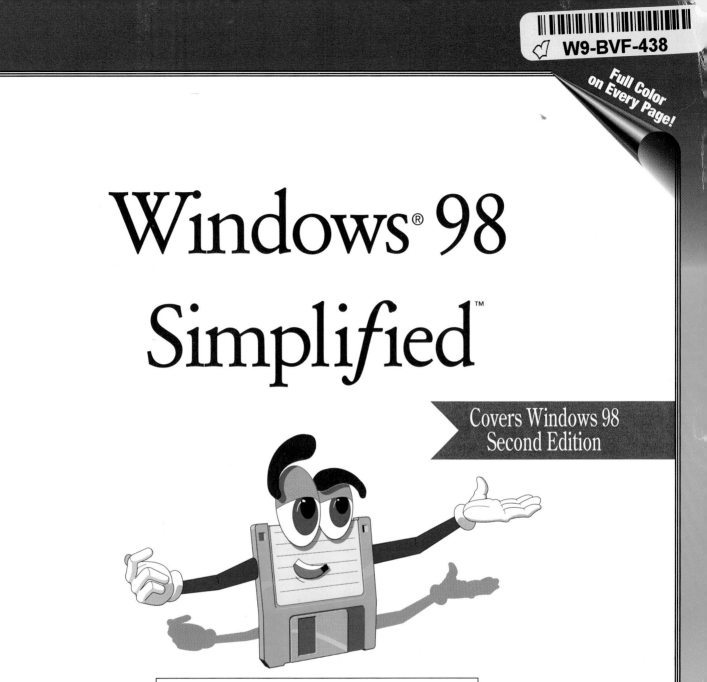

IDG's 3-D Visual™ Series

From
IDG BOOKS **maranGraphics™**

IDG Books Worldwide, Inc.
An International Data Group Company
Foster City, CA • Indianapolis • Chicago • New York

Windows® 98 Simplified™

Published by
IDG Books Worldwide, Inc.
An International Data Group Company
919 E. Hillsdale Blvd., Suite 400
Foster City, CA 94404
(650) 655-3000

Copyright© 1998 by maranGraphics Inc.
  5755 Coopers Avenue
  Mississauga, Ontario, Canada
  L4Z 1R9

Library of Congress Catalog Card No.: 98-84748
ISBN: 0-7645-6030-1
Printed in the United States of America
20 19 18 17 16 15 14

Distributed in the United States by IDG Books Worldwide, Inc.
Distributed by CDG Books Canada Inc. for Canada; by Transworld Publishers Limited in the United Kingdom; by IDG Norge Books for Norway; by IDG Sweden Books for Sweden; by IDG Books Australia Publishing Corporation Pty. Ltd. for Australia and New Zealand; by TransQuest Publishers Pte Ltd. for Singapore, Malaysia, Thailand, Indonesia, and Hong Kong; by Gotop Information Inc. for Taiwan; by ICG Muse, Inc. for Japan; by Norma Comunicaciones S.A. for Colombia; by Intersoft for South Africa; by Eyrolles for France; by International Thomson Publishing for Germany, Austria and Switzerland; by Distribuidora Cuspide for Argentina; by LR International for Brazil; by Galileo Libros for Chile; by Ediciones ZETA S.C.R. Ltda. for Peru; by WS Computer Publishing Corporation, Inc. for the Philippines; by Contemporanea de Ediciones for Venezuela; by Express Computer Distributors for the Caribbean and West Indies; by Micronesia Media Distributor, Inc. for Micronesia; by Grupo Editorial Norma S.A. for Guatemala; by Chips Computadoras S.A. de C.V. for Mexico; by Editorial Norma de Panama S.A. for Panama; by American Bookshops for Finland. Authorized Sales Agent: Anthony Rudkin Associates for the Middle East and North Africa.
For corporate orders, please call maranGraphics at 800-469-6616.
For general information on IDG Books Worldwide's books in the U.S., please call our Consumer Customer Service department at 800-762-2974.
For reseller information, including discounts and premium sales, please call our Reseller Customer Service department at 800-434-3422.
For information on where to purchase IDG Books Worldwide's books outside the U.S., please contact our International Sales department at 317-596-5530 or fax 317-596-5692.
For consumer information on foreign language translations, please contact our Customer Service department at 1-800-434-3422, fax 317-596-5692, or e-mail rights@idgbooks.com.
For information on licensing foreign or domestic rights, please phone 1-650-655-3109.
For sales inquiries and special prices for bulk quantities, please contact our Sales department at 650-655-3200.
For information on using IDG Books Worldwide's books in the classroom or for ordering examination copies, please contact our Educational Sales department at 800-434-2086 or fax 317-596-5499.
For press review copies, author interviews, or other publicity information, please contact our Public Relations department at 650-655-3000 or fax 650-655-3299.
For authorization to photocopy items for corporate, personal, or educational use, please contact maranGraphics at 800-469-6616.

Trademark Acknowledgments

Permissions

U.S. Corporate Sales	**U.S. Trade Sales**
Contact maranGraphics at (800) 469-6616 or fax (905) 890-9434.	Contact IDG Books at (800) 434-3422 or (650) 655-3000.

ABOUT IDG BOOKS WORLDWIDE

Welcome to the world of IDG Books Worldwide.

IDG Books Worldwide, Inc., is a subsidiary of International Data Group, the world's largest publisher of computer-related information and the leading global provider of information services on information technology. IDG was founded more than 30 years ago by Patrick J. McGovern and now employs more than 9,000 people worldwide. IDG publishes more than 290 computer publications in over 75 countries. More than 90 million people read one or more IDG publications each month.

Launched in 1990, IDG Books Worldwide is today the #1 publisher of best-selling computer books in the United States. We are proud to have received eight awards from the Computer Press Association in recognition of editorial excellence and three from Computer Currents' First Annual Readers' Choice Awards. Our best-selling ...*For Dummies®* series has more than 50 million copies in print with translations in 31 languages. IDG Books Worldwide, through a joint venture with IDG's Hi-Tech Beijing, became the first U.S. publisher to publish a computer book in the People's Republic of China. In record time, IDG Books Worldwide has become the first choice for millions of readers around the world who want to learn how to better manage their businesses.

Our mission is simple: Every one of our books is designed to bring extra value and skill-building instructions to the reader. Our books are written by experts who understand and care about our readers. The knowledge base of our editorial staff comes from years of experience in publishing, education, and journalism — experience we use to produce books to carry us into the new millennium. In short, we care about books, so we attract the best people. We devote special attention to details such as audience, interior design, use of icons, and illustrations. And because we use an efficient process of authoring, editing, and desktop publishing our books electronically, we can spend more time ensuring superior content and less time on the technicalities of making books.

You can count on our commitment to deliver high-quality books at competitive prices on topics you want to read about. At IDG Books Worldwide, we continue in the IDG tradition of delivering quality for more than 30 years. You'll find no better book on a subject than one from IDG Books Worldwide.

John Kilcullen
John Kilcullen
Chairman and CEO
IDG Books Worldwide, Inc.

Steven Berkowitz
Steven Berkowitz
President and Publisher
IDG Books Worldwide, Inc.

VIII
WINNER
Eighth Annual Computer Press Awards ≥ 1992

IX
WINNER
Ninth Annual Computer Press Awards ≥ 1993

X
WINNER
Tenth Annual Computer Press Awards ≥ 1994

XI
WINNER
Eleventh Annual Computer Press Awards ≥ 1995

IDG is the world's leading IT media, research and exposition company. Founded in 1964, IDG had 1997 revenues of $2.05 billion and has more than 9,000 employees worldwide. IDG offers the widest range of media options that reach IT buyers in 75 countries representing 95% of worldwide IT spending. IDG's diverse product and services portfolio spans six key areas including print publishing, online publishing, expositions and conferences, market research, education and training, and global marketing services. More than 90 million people read one or more of IDG's 290 magazines and newspapers, including IDG's leading global brands — Computerworld, PC World, Network World, Macworld and the Channel World family of publications. IDG Books Worldwide is one of the fastest-growing computer book publishers in the world, with more than 700 titles in 36 languages. The "...For Dummies®" series alone has more than 50 million copies in print. IDG offers online users the largest network of technology-specific Web sites around the world through IDG.net (http://www.idg.net), which comprises more than 225 targeted Web sites in 55 countries worldwide. International Data Corporation (IDC) is the world's largest provider of information technology data, analysis and consulting, with research centers in over 41 countries and more than 400 research analysts worldwide. IDG World Expo is a leading producer of more than 168 globally branded conferences and expositions in 35 countries including E3 (Electronic Entertainment Expo), Macworld Expo, ComNet, Windows World Expo, ICE (Internet Commerce Expo), Agenda, DEMO, and Spotlight. IDG's training subsidiary, ExecuTrain, is the world's largest computer training company, with more than 230 locations worldwide and 785 training courses. IDG Marketing Services helps industry-leading IT companies build international brand recognition by developing global integrated marketing programs via IDG's print, online and exposition products worldwide. Further information about the company can be found at www.idg.com. 1/24/99

maranGraphics is a family-run business located near Toronto, Canada.

At **maranGraphics**, we believe in producing great computer books—one book at a time.

Each maranGraphics book uses the award-winning communication process that we have been developing over the last 25 years. Using this process, we organize screen shots, text and illustrations in a way that makes it easy for you to learn new concepts and tasks.

We spend hours deciding the best way to perform each task, so you don't have to! Our clear, easy-to-follow screen shots and instructions walk you through each task from beginning to end.

Our detailed illustrations go hand-in-hand with the text to help reinforce the information. Each illustration is a labor of love—some take up to a week to draw!

We want to thank you for purchasing what we feel are the best computer books money can buy. We hope you enjoy using this book as much as we enjoyed creating it!

Sincerely,

The Maran Family

Please visit us on the Web at:
www.maran.com

Credits

Author & Architect:
Ruth Maran

Copy Development:
Wanda Lawrie

Second Edition Updates:
Kelleigh Wing
Roxanne Van Damme
Frances Lea
Cathy Benn

Project Manager:
Judy Maran

Editing & Screen Captures:
Raquel Scott
Janice Boyer
Michelle Kirchner
James Menzies
Stacey Morrison

Screen Artist:
Jimmy Tam

Layout Designers & Illustrators:
Jamie Bell
Treena Lees

Illustrators:
Russ Marini
Peter Grecco
Sean Johannesen
Steven Schaerer

Permissions Coordinator:
Jenn Hillman

Indexer:
Kelleigh Wing

Post Production:
Robert Maran

Editorial Support:
Barry Pruett
Martine Edwards

Acknowledgments

Thanks to the dedicated staff of maranGraphics, including
Jamie Bell, Cathy Benn, Janice Boyer, Peter Grecco,
Jenn Hillman, Sean Johannesen, Michelle Kirchner, Wanda
Lawrie, Francis Lea, Treena Lees, Jill Maran, Judy Maran,
Robert Maran, Sherry Maran, Russ Marini, James Menzies,
Stacey Morrison, Steven Schaerer, Raquel Scott, Jimmy Tam,
Roxanne Van Damme, Paul Whitehead and Kelleigh Wing.

Finally, to Richard Maran who originated the easy-to-use graphic
format of this guide. Thank you for your inspiration and guidance.

Table of Contents

CHAPTER 3

Create Pictures

CHAPTER 4

View Files

CHAPTER 5

Work With Files

CHAPTER 6

Customize Windows

Table of Contents

CHAPTER 7

Have Fun with Windows

CHAPTER 8

Optimize Your Computer

CHAPTER 9

Browse the Web

CHAPTER 11

Work with Channels

CHAPTER 10

Exchange Electronic Mail

Microsoft® Windows® 98 is a program that controls the overall activity of your computer.

Windows ensures that all parts of your computer work together smoothly and efficiently.

Work with Files

Windows provides ways to organize and manage the files stored on your computer. You can open, sort, rename, move, print, find and delete files.

Write Letters and Draw Pictures

Windows includes a word processing program, called WordPad, which you can use to write letters. Windows also includes a drawing program, called Paint, which you can use to draw pictures.

Customize Windows

You can customize Windows in many ways. You can add a colorful design to your screen, change the way your mouse works and change the amount of information that fits on the screen.

Have Fun with Windows

You can have fun with Windows. You can play games, play music CDs and assign sounds to program events.

Optimize Your Computer

Windows provides tools to help you optimize your computer. You can check your hard disk for errors, remove unnecessary files and defragment your hard disk to improve its performance.

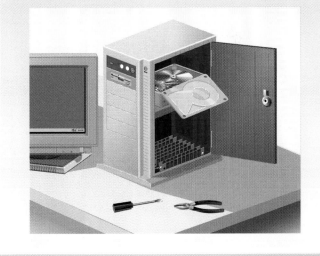

Exchange Electronic Mail

Windows includes a program that allows you to exchange electronic mail with people around the world. You can exchange messages with friends, colleagues, family members and clients.

Browse the Web

Windows lets you browse through the information on the World Wide Web. You can access information on any subject imaginable. You can review magazines, encyclopedias, travel guides, famous speeches, recipes, job listings, airline schedules and much more.

There are currently two versions of Windows 98. You may have the original version or Windows 98 Second Edition installed on your computer.

Windows 98 Second Edition includes many enhancements and updates to the original version of Windows 98.

Determine Your Version

You can check your Windows 98 CD-ROM disc to see which version is installed on your computer. If you purchased Windows 98 before May 1999, you probably have the original version of Windows 98. If you purchased Windows 98 after May 1999, you probably have Windows 98 Second Edition.

Upgrade Windows 98

If you have the original version of Windows 98, there are many individual features you can add to upgrade the program, such as security and year 2000 updates. You can download each product update from the following Web site:

windowsupdate.microsoft.com

If you want to upgrade the entire original version to Windows 98 Second Edition, you can order Windows 98 Second Edition from the following Web site:

www.microsoft.com/windows98

Internet Explorer 5

Windows 98 Second Edition includes a new version of Internet Explorer. Internet Explorer 5 provides updated features for browsing the Web, such as a search feature that makes it easier to find Web pages of interest.

Outlook Express 5

Outlook Express 5 is included with Internet Explorer 5 in Windows 98 Second Edition. This updated version of Outlook Express provides enhanced features for exchanging e-mail messages, such as a contacts list that makes it easier to send messages to friends and colleagues.

Share an Internet Connection on a Network

A network is a group of connected computers that allow people to share information and equipment. Windows 98 Second Edition includes an Internet Connection Sharing feature, which allows several computers on a network to use one modem or high-speed connection to access the Internet at the same time.

Channels

Channels are specially designed Web sites that Windows can automatically deliver to your computer. Depending on the way you upgraded to Windows 98 Second Edition, you may not have access to channels.

The Windows 98 screen displays various items. The items that appear depend on how your computer is set up and the version of Windows 98 you are using.

My Computer

Lets you view all the folders and files stored on your computer.

My Documents

Provides a convenient place to store your documents.

Network Neighborhood

Lets you view all the folders and files available on your network.

Recycle Bin

Stores deleted files and allows you to recover them later.

Quick Launch Toolbar

Gives you quick access to commonly used features, including Internet Explorer, Outlook Express, the desktop and channels.

Title Bar

Displays the name of an open window.

Window

A rectangle on your screen that displays information.

Desktop

The background area of your screen.

Channel Bar

Displays special Web sites that Windows can automatically deliver to your computer.

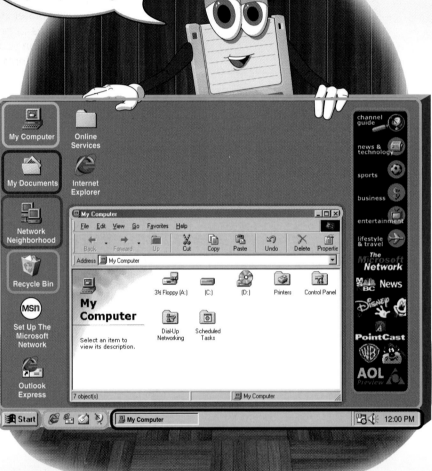

Start Button

Gives you quick access to programs, files and Windows Help.

Taskbar

Displays a button for each open window on your screen. You can use these buttons to switch between the open windows.

A mouse is a handheld device that lets you select and move items on your screen.

When you move the mouse on your desk, the mouse pointer on your screen moves in the same direction. The mouse pointer assumes different shapes, such as $\hbox{$\k$}$ or I, depending on its location on your screen and the task you are performing.

Resting your hand on the mouse, use your thumb and two rightmost fingers to move the mouse on your desk. Use your two remaining fingers to press the mouse buttons.

MOUSE ACTIONS

Click
Press and release the left mouse button.

Double-click
Quickly press and release the left mouse button twice.

Right-click
Press and release the right mouse button.

Drag
Position the mouse pointer over an object on your screen and then press and hold down the left mouse button. Still holding down the button, move the mouse to where you want to place the object and then release the button.

Windows provides an easy, graphical way for you to use your computer. Windows starts when you turn on your computer.

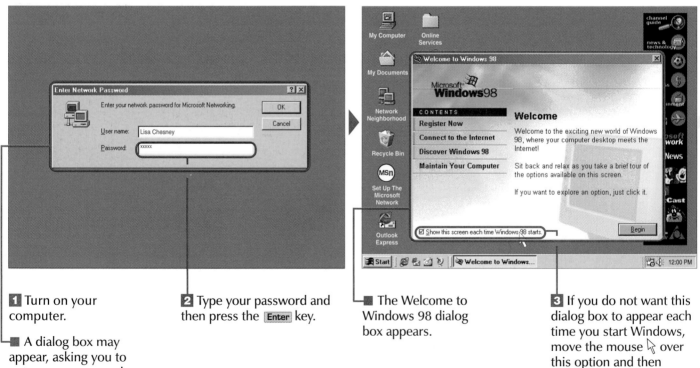

1 Turn on your computer.

■ A dialog box may appear, asking you to enter your password.

2 Type your password and then press the `Enter` key.

■ The Welcome to Windows 98 dialog box appears.

3 If you do not want this dialog box to appear each time you start Windows, move the mouse ⟍ over this option and then press the left button (☑ changes to ☐).

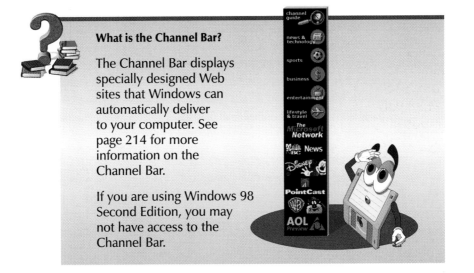

What is the Channel Bar?

The Channel Bar displays specially designed Web sites that Windows can automatically deliver to your computer. See page 214 for more information on the Channel Bar.

If you are using Windows 98 Second Edition, you may not have access to the Channel Bar.

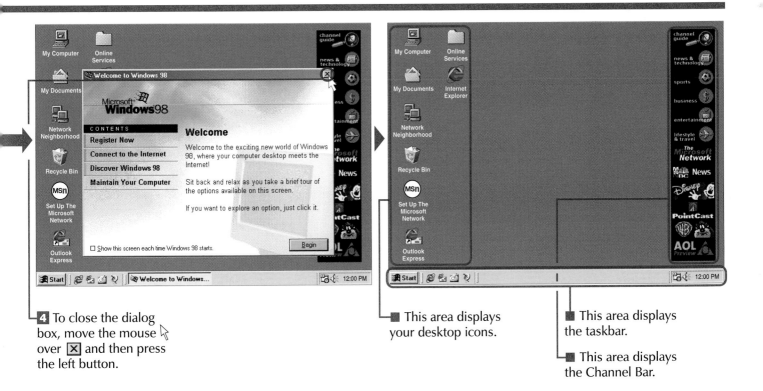

◢**4** To close the dialog box, move the mouse over ⊠ and then press the left button.

■ This area displays your desktop icons.

■ This area displays the taskbar.

■ This area displays the Channel Bar.

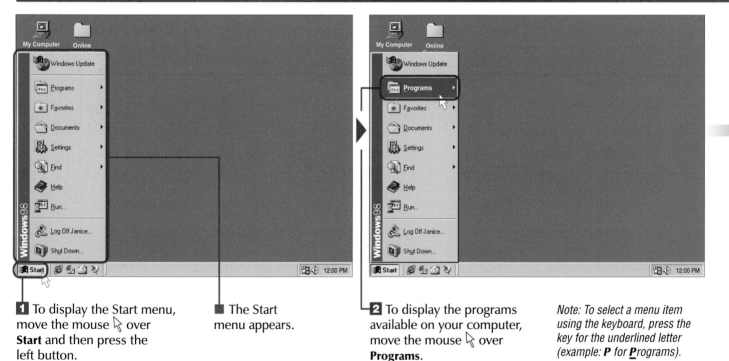

1 To display the Start menu, move the mouse ⤢ over **Start** and then press the left button.

Note: To display the Start menu using the keyboard, press and hold down the Ctrl *key and then press the* Esc *key.*

■ The Start menu appears.

2 To display the programs available on your computer, move the mouse ⤢ over **Programs**.

*Note: To select a menu item using the keyboard, press the key for the underlined letter (example: **P** for **P**rograms).*

Which programs does Windows provide?

Windows comes with many useful programs.

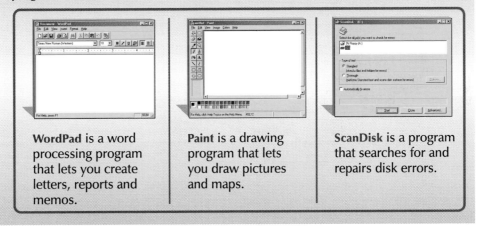

WordPad is a word processing program that lets you create letters, reports and memos.

Paint is a drawing program that lets you draw pictures and maps.

ScanDisk is a program that searches for and repairs disk errors.

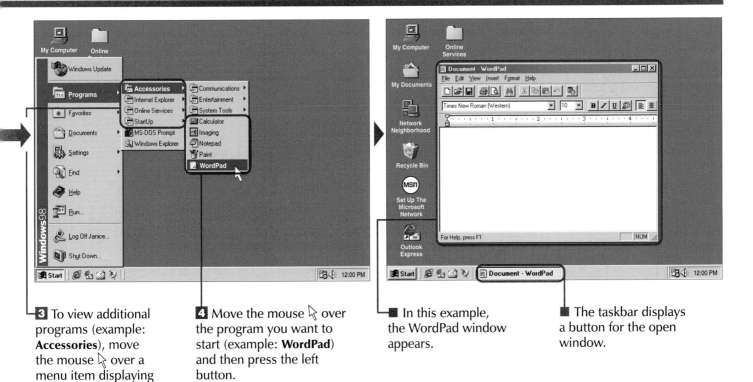

3 To view additional programs (example: **Accessories**), move the mouse ⌖ over a menu item displaying an arrow (▶).

4 Move the mouse ⌖ over the program you want to start (example: **WordPad**) and then press the left button.

Note: To close the Start menu without selecting a program, move the mouse ⌖ outside the menu area and then press the left button.

■ In this example, the WordPad window appears.

■ The taskbar displays a button for the open window.

You can enlarge a window to fill your screen. This lets you view more of the window's contents.

MAXIMIZE A WINDOW

1 Move the mouse ▷ over ▢ in the window you want to maximize and then press the left mouse button.

■ The window fills your screen.

■ To return the window to its previous size, move the mouse ▷ over ▣ and then press the left button.

If you are not using a window, you can minimize the window to remove it from your screen. You can redisplay the window at any time.

MINIMIZE A WINDOW

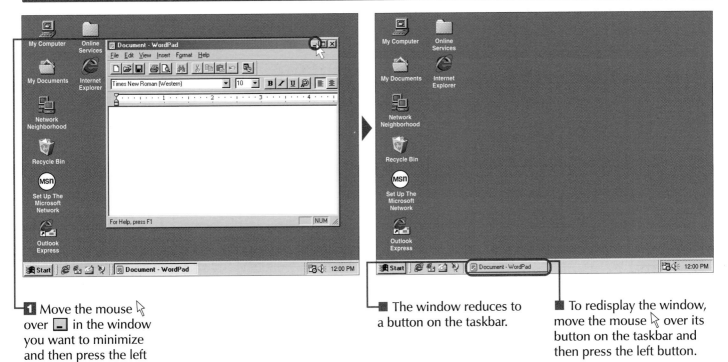

1 Move the mouse ⬚ over ⬚ in the window you want to minimize and then press the left button.

■ The window reduces to a button on the taskbar.

■ To redisplay the window, move the mouse ⬚ over its button on the taskbar and then press the left button.

If a window covers items on your screen, you can move the window to a different location.

MOVE A WINDOW

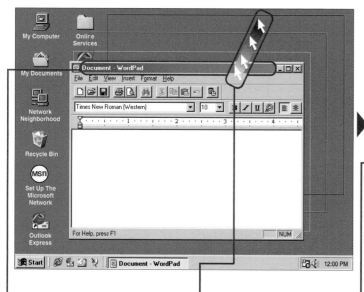

1 Position the mouse ⬚ over the title bar of the window you want to move.

2 Press and hold down the left button as you drag the mouse ⬚ to where you want to place the window.

■ The window moves to the new location.

You can easily change the size of a window displayed on your screen.

Enlarging a window lets you view more of its contents. Reducing a window lets you view items covered by the window.

SIZE A WINDOW

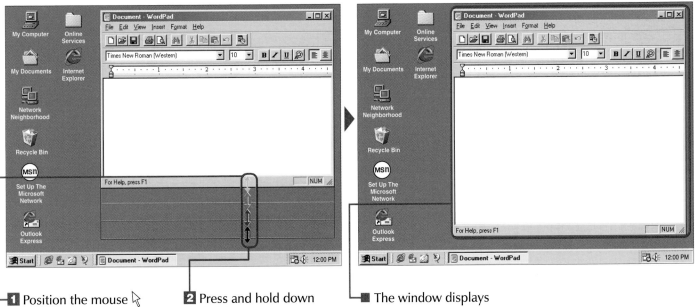

1 Position the mouse ⊾ over an edge of the window you want to size (⊾ changes to ↕, ↔ or ↘).

2 Press and hold down the left button as you drag the mouse ↕ until the window displays the size you want.

■ The window displays the new size.

You can use a scroll bar to browse through the information in a window. This is useful when a window is not large enough to display all the information it contains.

SCROLL DOWN

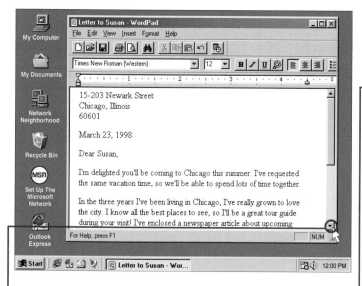

1 To scroll down through the information in a window, move the mouse ↖ over ▼ and then press the left button.

SCROLL UP

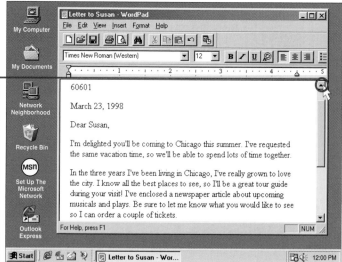

1 To scroll up through the information in a window, move the mouse ↖ over ▲ and then press the left button.

Is there another way to use a mouse to scroll through a window?

You can purchase a mouse with a wheel between the left and right mouse buttons. Moving this wheel lets you scroll through a window.

SCROLL TO ANY POSITION

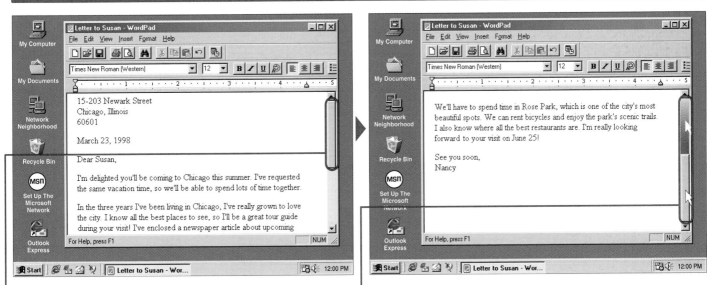

■ The location of the scroll box indicates which part of the window you are viewing. For example, when the scroll box is halfway down the scroll bar, you are viewing information from the middle of the window.

Note: The size of the scroll box varies, depending on the amount of information the window contains.

■1 Press and hold down the left button as you drag the scroll box along the scroll bar until the information you want to view appears.

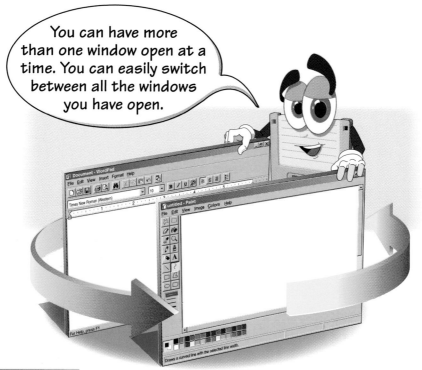

You can have more than one window open at a time. You can easily switch between all the windows you have open.

Each window is like a separate piece of paper. Switching between windows lets you place a different piece of paper at the top of the pile.

SWITCH BETWEEN WINDOWS

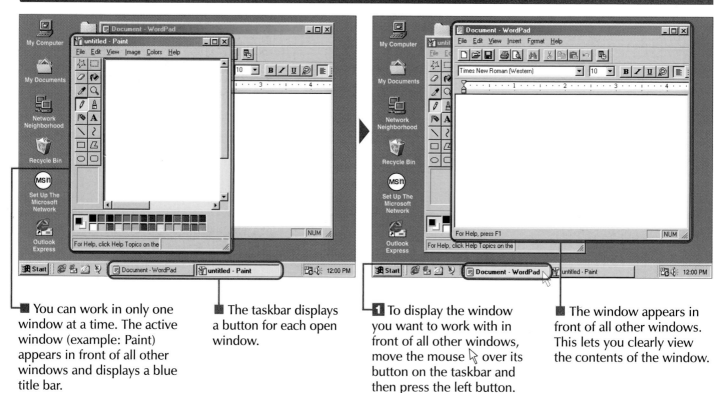

■ You can work in only one window at a time. The active window (example: Paint) appears in front of all other windows and displays a blue title bar.

■ The taskbar displays a button for each open window.

1 To display the window you want to work with in front of all other windows, move the mouse ⬚ over its button on the taskbar and then press the left button.

■ The window appears in front of all other windows. This lets you clearly view the contents of the window.

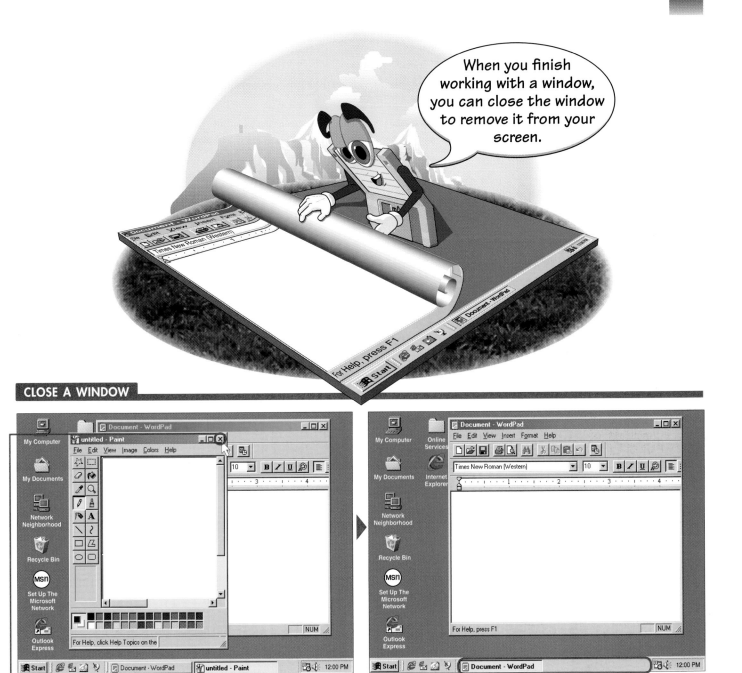

When you finish working with a window, you can close the window to remove it from your screen.

CLOSE A WINDOW

1 Move the mouse ⬚ over ✗ in the window you want to close and then press the left button.

■ The window disappears from your screen.

■ The button for the window disappears from the taskbar.

You can instantly minimize all your open windows to remove them from your screen. This allows you to clearly view the desktop.

SHOW THE DESKTOP

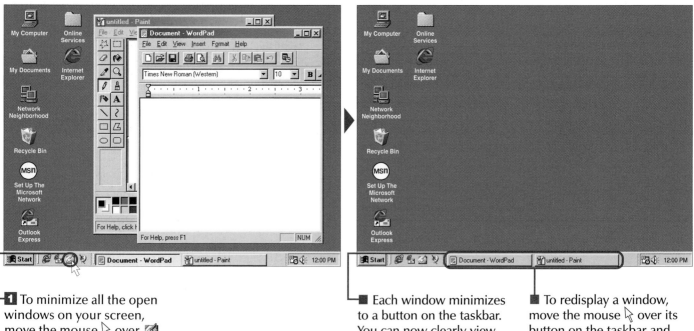

1 To minimize all the open windows on your screen, move the mouse ⟋ over 🖌 and then press the left button.

■ Each window minimizes to a button on the taskbar. You can now clearly view the desktop.

■ To redisplay a window, move the mouse ⟋ over its button on the taskbar and then press the left button.

SHUT DOWN WINDOWS

When you finish using your computer, you should shut down Windows before turning off the computer.

■ Do not turn off your computer until this message appears on your screen.

SHUT DOWN WINDOWS

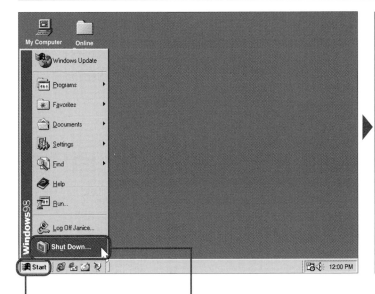

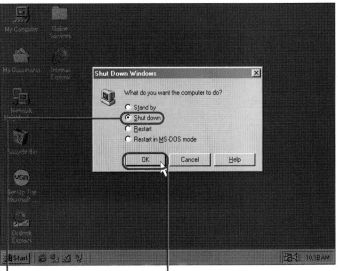

1 Move the mouse ⟨ over **Start** and then press the left button.

2 Move the mouse ⟨ over **Shut Down** and then press the left button.

■ The Shut Down Windows dialog box appears.

3 Move the mouse ⟨ over **Shut down** and then press the left button (○ changes to ⊙).

4 To shut down your computer, move the mouse ⟨ over **OK** and then press the left button.

If you do not know how to perform a task, you can use the Help feature to get information.

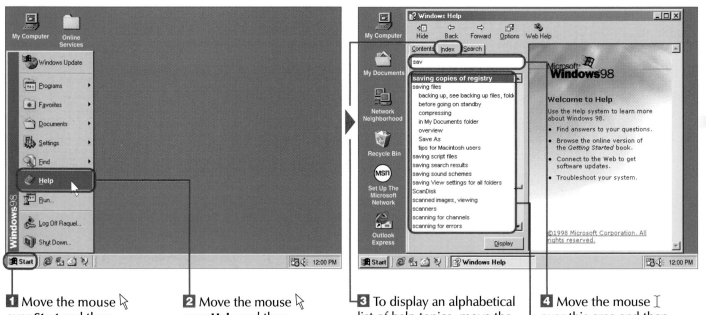

1 Move the mouse over **Start** and then press the left button.

2 Move the mouse over **Help** and then press the left button.

■ The Windows Help window appears.

3 To display an alphabetical list of help topics, move the mouse over the **Index** tab and then press the left button.

4 Move the mouse over this area and then press the left button. Type the first few letters of the topic of interest.

■ This area displays help topics beginning with the letters you typed.

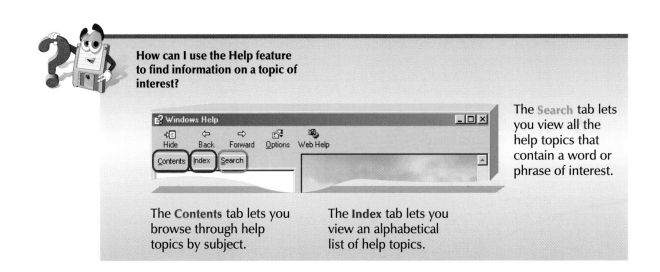

How can I use the Help feature to find information on a topic of interest?

The **Search** tab lets you view all the help topics that contain a word or phrase of interest.

The **Contents** tab lets you browse through help topics by subject.

The **Index** tab lets you view an alphabetical list of help topics.

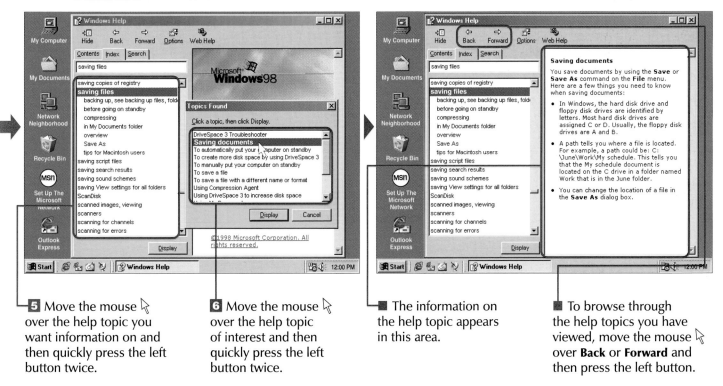

5 Move the mouse over the help topic you want information on and then quickly press the left button twice.

■ The Topics Found dialog box may appear, displaying a list of related help topics.

6 Move the mouse over the help topic of interest and then quickly press the left button twice.

■ The information on the help topic appears in this area.

■ To browse through the help topics you have viewed, move the mouse over **Back** or **Forward** and then press the left button.

CHAPTER 2

CREATE DOCUMENTS

Do you want to create documents such as letters and memos? In this chapter you will learn how to create documents quickly and efficiently using the WordPad program.

> WordPad allows you to create simple documents, such as letters and memos.

START WORDPAD

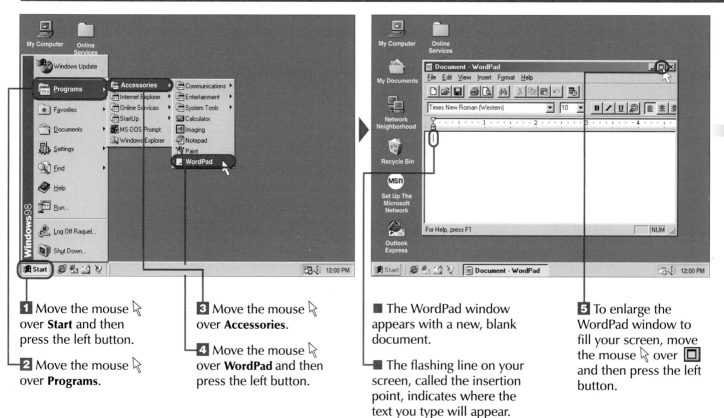

1 Move the mouse ⟨ over **Start** and then press the left button.

2 Move the mouse ⟨ over **Programs**.

3 Move the mouse ⟨ over **Accessories**.

4 Move the mouse ⟨ over **WordPad** and then press the left button.

■ The WordPad window appears with a new, blank document.

■ The flashing line on your screen, called the insertion point, indicates where the text you type will appear.

5 To enlarge the WordPad window to fill your screen, move the mouse ⟨ over ▢ and then press the left button.

26

Does WordPad offer all the features I need?

WordPad is a simple program that offers only basic word processing features. If you need more advanced features, you can purchase a more powerful word processor, such as Microsoft Word or Corel WordPerfect. These programs include features such as tables, graphics, a spell checker and a thesaurus.

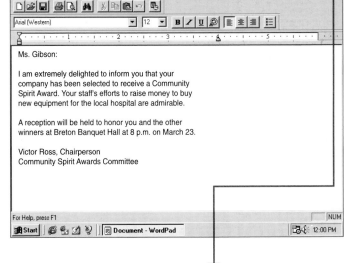

6 Type the text for your document.

■ When you reach the end of a line, WordPad automatically moves the text to the next line. You only need to press the `Enter` key when you want to start a new line or paragraph.

Note: To make the example easier to read, the font type and size have been changed. To change the font type and size, see page 36.

When you finish using WordPad, you can exit the program.

1 Before exiting WordPad, save any changes you made to the document. To save your changes, see page 32.

2 To exit WordPad, move the mouse ⬚ over ☒ and then press the left button.

You can easily add new text to your document and remove text you no longer need.

INSERT TEXT

1 Move the mouse I over the location where you want to insert text and then press the left button.

■ The flashing insertion point indicates where the text you type will appear.

2 Type the text you want to insert.

3 To insert a blank space, press the Spacebar.

Note: The words to the right of the new text move forward.

28

How do I cancel changes I made?

WordPad remembers the last changes you made to your document. If you regret a change, you can cancel the change by using the Undo feature.

1 To undo your last change, move the mouse ⏴ over ↶ and then press the left button. You can repeat this step to undo previous changes.

DELETE TEXT

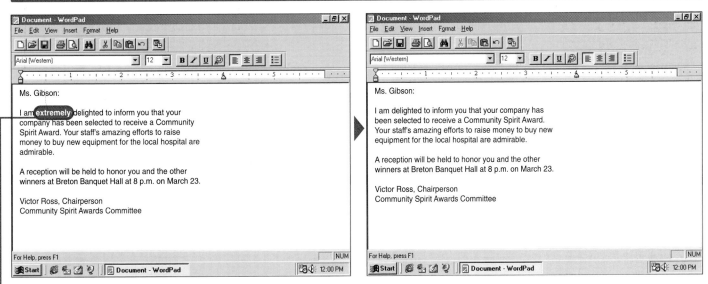

1 To select the text you want to delete, press and hold down the left button as you drag the mouse I over the text until the text is highlighted.

2 Press the Delete key to remove the text.

■ To delete one character at a time, move the mouse I to the left of the first character you want to delete and then press the left button. Press the Delete key for each character you want to remove.

> You can reorganize your document by moving text from one location to another.

MOVE TEXT

1 To select the text you want to move, press and hold down the left button as you drag the mouse I over the text until the text is highlighted.

2 Move the mouse ⌖ over ✂ to move the text and then press the left button.

■ The text you selected disappears from your screen.

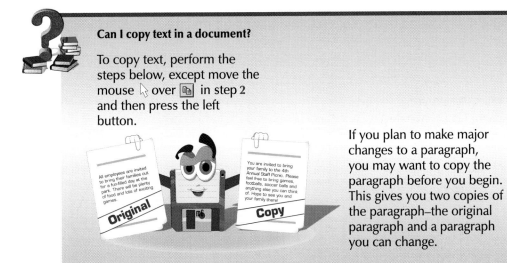

Can I copy text in a document?

To copy text, perform the steps below, except move the mouse ⍦ over 🖹 in step 2 and then press the left button.

All employees are invited to bring their families out for a fun-filled day at the park. There will be plenty of food and lots of exciting games.

Original

You are invited to bring your family to the 4th Annual Staff Picnic. Please feel free to bring games, footballs, soccer balls and anything else you can think of. Hope to see you and your family there!

Copy

If you plan to make major changes to a paragraph, you may want to copy the paragraph before you begin. This gives you two copies of the paragraph–the original paragraph and a paragraph you can change.

---

3 Move the mouse I over the location where you want to place the text and then press the left button. The flashing insertion point indicates where the text will appear.

4 Move the mouse ⍦ over 🖹 and then press the left button.

■ The text appears in the new location.

You should save your document to store it for future use. This lets you later retrieve the document for reviewing or editing.

You should regularly save changes you make to a document to avoid losing your work.

SAVE A DOCUMENT

1 Move the mouse over 🖫 to save the document and then press the left button.

■ The Save As dialog box appears.

Note: If you previously saved the document, the Save As dialog box will not appear since you have already named the document.

2 Type a name for the document.

■ This area shows the location where WordPad will store the document.

3 Move the mouse over **Save** and then press the left button.

PRINT A DOCUMENT

You can produce a paper copy of the document displayed on your screen.

PRINT A DOCUMENT

1 Move the mouse over **File** and then press the left button.

2 Move the mouse over **Print** and then press the left button.

■ The Print dialog box appears.

3 To print the document, move the mouse over **OK** and then press the left button.

You can open a saved document and display the document on your screen. This allows you to view and make changes to the document.

OPEN A DOCUMENT

1 To open a document, move the mouse ⬚ over ⬚ and then press the left button.

■ The Open dialog box appears.

■ This area shows the location of the displayed documents.

2 Move the mouse ⬚ over the name of the document you want to open and then press the left button.

Note: If you cannot find the document you want to open, see page 92 to find the document.

3 Move the mouse ⬚ over **Open** and then press the left button.

Can I work with two WordPad documents open at the same time?

WordPad only lets you work with one document at a time. If you are currently working with a document, save the document before opening another. For information on saving a document, see page 32.

QUICKLY OPEN A DOCUMENT

■ WordPad opens the document and displays it on your screen. You can now review and make changes to the document.

The File menu displays the names of the last four documents you opened.

1 To quickly open a document, move the mouse over **File** and then press the left button.

2 Move the mouse over the name of the document you want to open and then press the left button.

You can enhance the appearance of your document by changing the design of the text.

CHANGE FONT TYPE

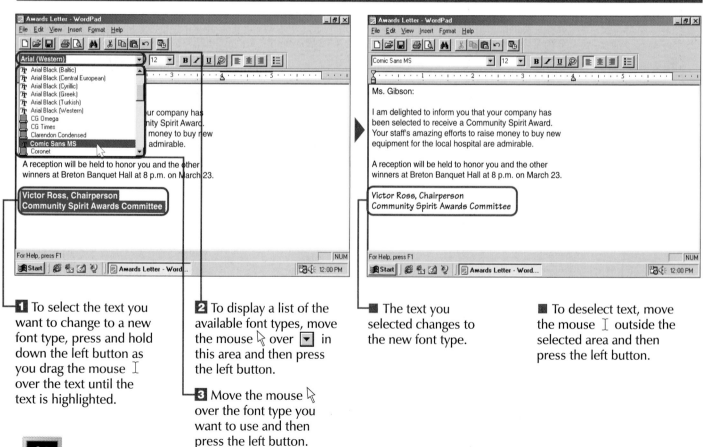

1 To select the text you want to change to a new font type, press and hold down the left button as you drag the mouse I over the text until the text is highlighted.

2 To display a list of the available font types, move the mouse ↖ over ▾ in this area and then press the left button.

3 Move the mouse ↖ over the font type you want to use and then press the left button.

■ The text you selected changes to the new font type.

■ To deselect text, move the mouse I outside the selected area and then press the left button.

CHANGE FONT SIZE

CHANGE FONT SIZE

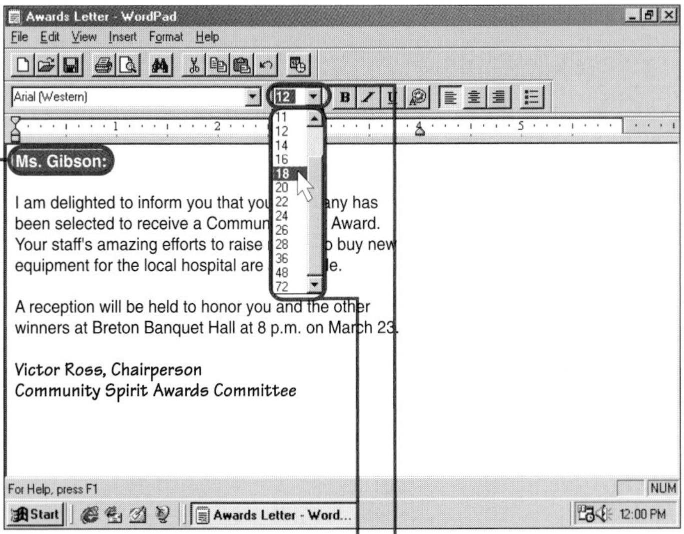

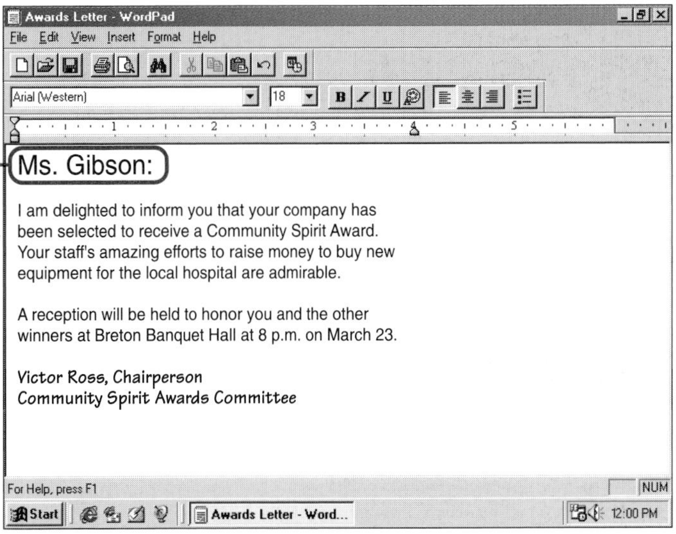

1 To select the text you want to change to a new font size, press and hold down the left button as you drag the mouse I over the text until the text is highlighted.

2 To display a list of the available font sizes, move the mouse over ▼ in this area and then press the left button.

3 Move the mouse over the font size you want to use and then press the left button.

■ The text you selected changes to the new font size.

■ To deselect text, move the mouse I outside the selected area and then press the left button.

You can use the Bold, Italic and Underline features to emphasize important information in your document.

1 To select the text you want to change to a new style, press and hold down the left button as you drag the mouse I over the text until the text is highlighted.

2 Move the mouse ⍦ over one of the following styles and then press the left button.

B Bold

I Italic

U Underline

■ The text you selected appears in the new style.

■ To deselect text, move the mouse I outside the selected area and then press the left button.

■ To remove a bold, italic or underline style, repeat steps **1** and **2**.

CHANGE ALIGNMENT OF TEXT

You can make your document look more attractive by aligning text in different ways.
Right Align
Harry's Auto Center
23 Duke Street
New York, NY
10023
Offering a Wide Range of Services for All Car Models
Center
Tune-up
Tire rotation
Oil check
Rust protection
Brake inspection and repair
Fluid leakage detection
Exhaust system repair
Left Align

CHANGE ALIGNMENT OF TEXT

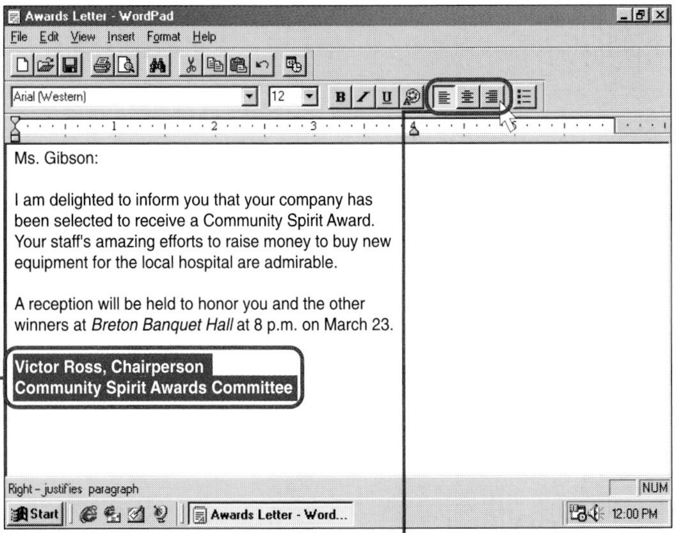
Awards Letter - WordPad
File Edit View Insert Format Help
Arial (Western)
12
Ms. Gibson:
I am delighted to inform you that your company has been selected to receive a Community Spirit Award. Your staff's amazing efforts to raise money to buy new equipment for the local hospital are admirable.
A reception will be held to honor you and the other winners at Breton Banquet Hall at 8 p.m. on March 23.
Victor Ross, Chairperson
Community Spirit Awards Committee
Right - justifies paragraph
NUM
Start
Awards Letter - Word...
12:00 PM

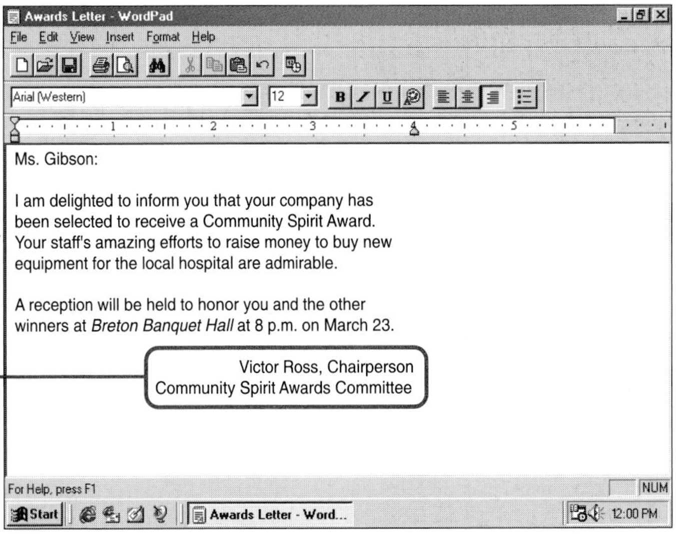
Awards Letter - WordPad
File Edit View Insert Format Help
Arial (Western)
12
Ms. Gibson:
I am delighted to inform you that your company has been selected to receive a Community Spirit Award. Your staff's amazing efforts to raise money to buy new equipment for the local hospital are admirable.
A reception will be held to honor you and the other winners at Breton Banquet Hall at 8 p.m. on March 23.
Victor Ross, Chairperson
Community Spirit Awards Committee
For Help, press F1
NUM
Start
Awards Letter - Word...
12:00 PM

1 To select the text you want to align differently, press and hold down the left button as you drag the mouse I over the text until the text is highlighted.

2 Move the mouse over one of the following options and then press the left button.

- Left align
- Center
- Right align

■ The text displays the new alignment.

■ To deselect text, move the mouse I outside the selected area and then press the left button.

CHAPTER 3

CREATE PICTURES

Can I use my artistic abilities on my computer? In this chapter you will learn how to create pictures using the Paint program.

You can use Paint to draw pictures and maps on your computer.

START PAINT

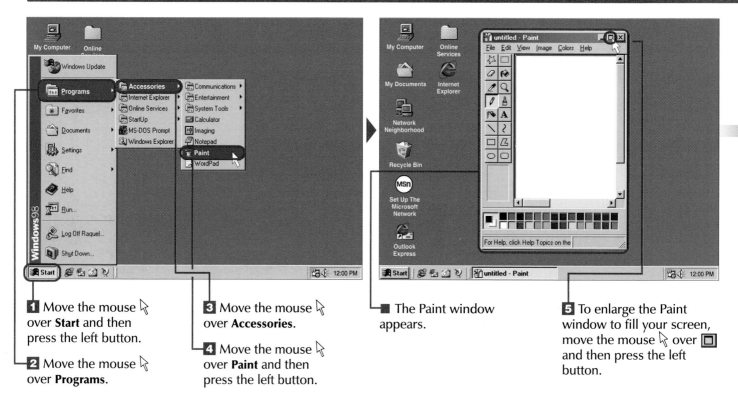

1 Move the mouse ⩗ over **Start** and then press the left button.

2 Move the mouse ⩗ over **Programs**.

3 Move the mouse ⩗ over **Accessories**.

4 Move the mouse ⩗ over **Paint** and then press the left button.

■ The Paint window appears.

5 To enlarge the Paint window to fill your screen, move the mouse ⩗ over 🔲 and then press the left button.

What can I do with the pictures I draw in Paint?

You can place the pictures you draw in Paint in other programs. For example, you can add your company logo to a business letter you created in WordPad.

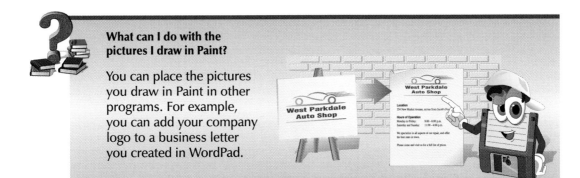

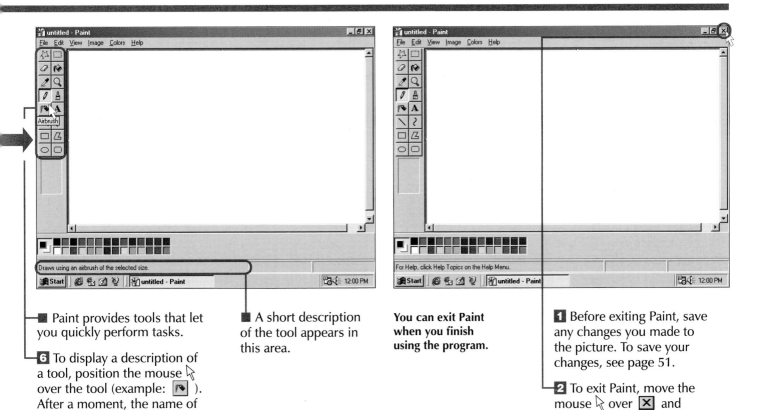

■ Paint provides tools that let you quickly perform tasks.

6 To display a description of a tool, position the mouse over the tool (example:). After a moment, the name of the tool appears.

■ A short description of the tool appears in this area.

You can exit Paint when you finish using the program.

1 Before exiting Paint, save any changes you made to the picture. To save your changes, see page 51.

2 To exit Paint, move the mouse over and then press the left button.

DRAW SHAPES

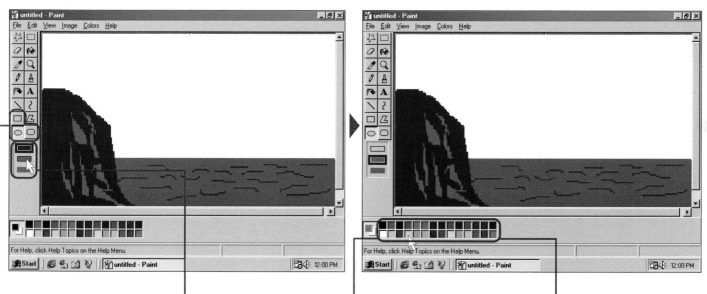

1 Move the mouse ⯅ over the tool for the type of shape you want to draw (example: ⬭) and then press the left button.

2 To select how you want to draw the shape, move the mouse ⯅ over one of the options in this area and then press the left button.

Note: For more information, see the top of page 45.

3 To select a color for the outline of the shape, move the mouse ⯅ over the color (example: ▮) and then press the left button.

4 To select a color for the inside of the shape, move the mouse ⯅ over the color (example: ▯) and then press the **right** button.

How can I draw a shape?

Paint offers three ways to draw a shape.

Draws the outline of a shape.

Draws the outline of a shape and fills the inside with color.

Draws a colored shape without an outline.

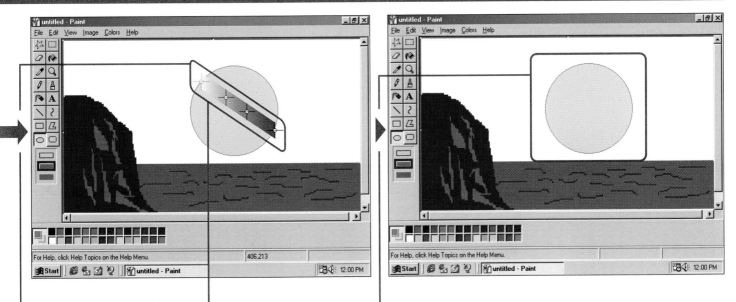

5 Position the mouse ☌ where you want to begin drawing the shape (☌ changes to ┼).

6 Press and hold down the left button as you drag the mouse ┼ until the shape is the size you want.

Note: To draw a perfect circle or square, press and hold down the **Shift** *key as you perform step 6.*

■ The shape appears.

DRAW LINES

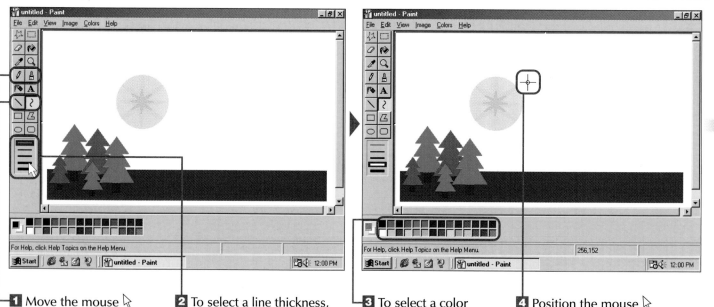

1 Move the mouse ▷ over the tool for the type of line you want to draw (example: ⟨?⟩) and then press the left button.

Note: For more information, see the top of page 47.

2 To select a line thickness, move the mouse ▷ over one of the options in this area and then press the left button.

Note: The ⟨∕⟩ tool does not provide any line thickness options. The ⟨A⟩ tool provides a different set of options.

3 To select a color for the line, move the mouse ▷ over the color (example: ▇) and then press the left button.

4 Position the mouse ▷ where you want to begin drawing the line (▷ changes to ┼, ∕ or ┼).

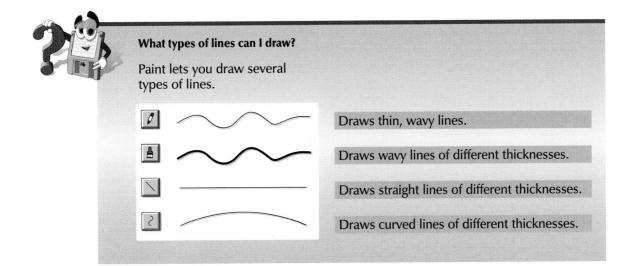

What types of lines can I draw?

Paint lets you draw several types of lines.

Draws thin, wavy lines.

Draws wavy lines of different thicknesses.

Draws straight lines of different thicknesses.

Draws curved lines of different thicknesses.

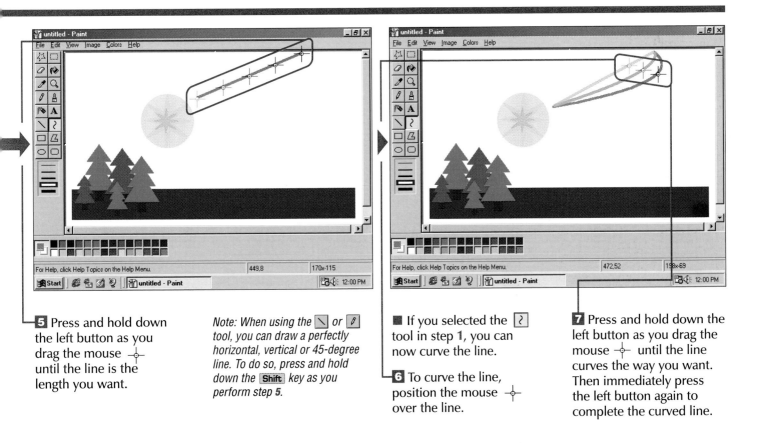

5 Press and hold down the left button as you drag the mouse ✛ until the line is the length you want.

Note: When using the ＼ or ✎ tool, you can draw a perfectly horizontal, vertical or 45-degree line. To do so, press and hold down the **Shift** *key as you perform step* **5**.

■ If you selected the ? tool in step **1**, you can now curve the line.

6 To curve the line, position the mouse ✛ over the line.

7 Press and hold down the left button as you drag the mouse ✛ until the line curves the way you want. Then immediately press the left button again to complete the curved line.

You can add text to your picture, such as a title or explanation.

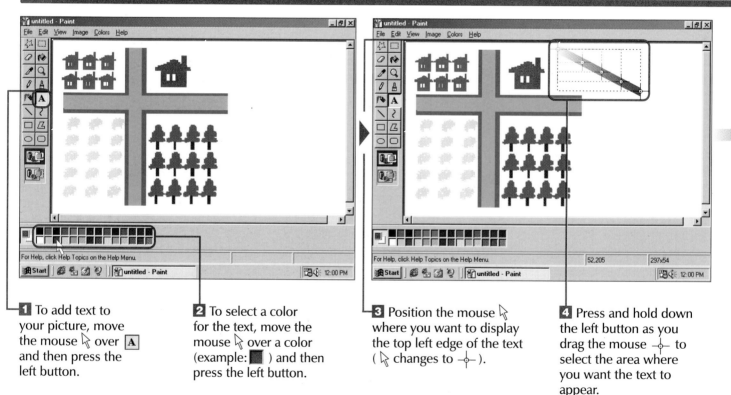

1 To add text to your picture, move the mouse over **A** and then press the left button.

2 To select a color for the text, move the mouse over a color (example: ■) and then press the left button.

3 Position the mouse where you want to display the top left edge of the text (changes to ⊹).

4 Press and hold down the left button as you drag the mouse ⊹ to select the area where you want the text to appear.

■ A dotted box appears.

How do I display the Text Toolbar on my screen?

If the Text Toolbar does not appear when adding text to a picture, you can easily display the toolbar.

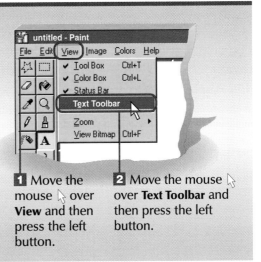

1 Move the mouse over **View** and then press the left button.

2 Move the mouse over **Text Toolbar** and then press the left button.

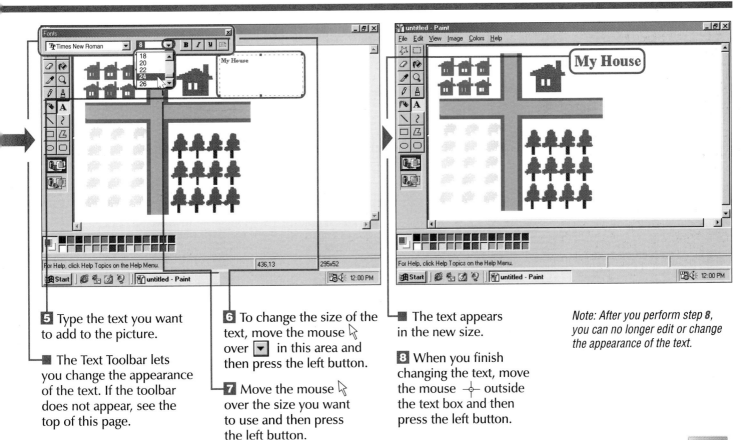

5 Type the text you want to add to the picture.

■ The Text Toolbar lets you change the appearance of the text. If the toolbar does not appear, see the top of this page.

6 To change the size of the text, move the mouse over ▼ in this area and then press the left button.

7 Move the mouse over the size you want to use and then press the left button.

■ The text appears in the new size.

8 When you finish changing the text, move the mouse outside the text box and then press the left button.

Note: After you perform step 8, you can no longer edit or change the appearance of the text.

You can use the Eraser tool to remove part of your picture.

When choosing a color for the eraser, select a color that matches the background color of your picture.

ERASE PART OF A PICTURE

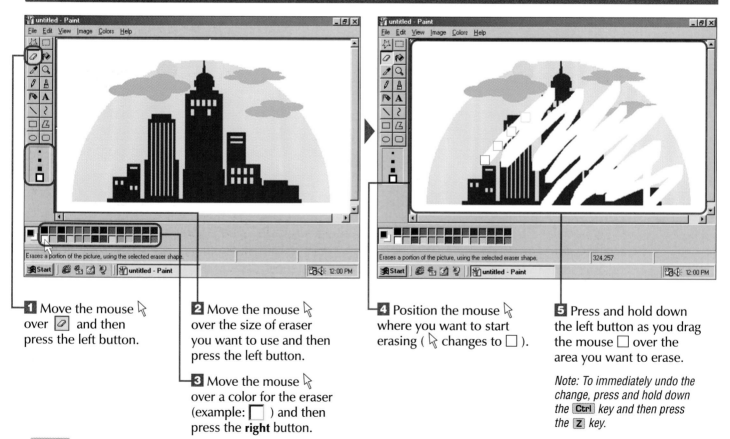

1 Move the mouse ☒ over ⬚ and then press the left button.

2 Move the mouse ☒ over the size of eraser you want to use and then press the left button.

3 Move the mouse ☒ over a color for the eraser (example: ⬚) and then press the **right** button.

4 Position the mouse ☒ where you want to start erasing (☒ changes to ⬚).

5 Press and hold down the left button as you drag the mouse ⬚ over the area you want to erase.

Note: To immediately undo the change, press and hold down the **Ctrl** *key and then press the* **Z** *key.*

You should save your picture to store the picture for future use. This lets you later review and make changes to the picture.

You should regularly save changes you make to a picture to avoid losing your work.

SAVE A PICTURE

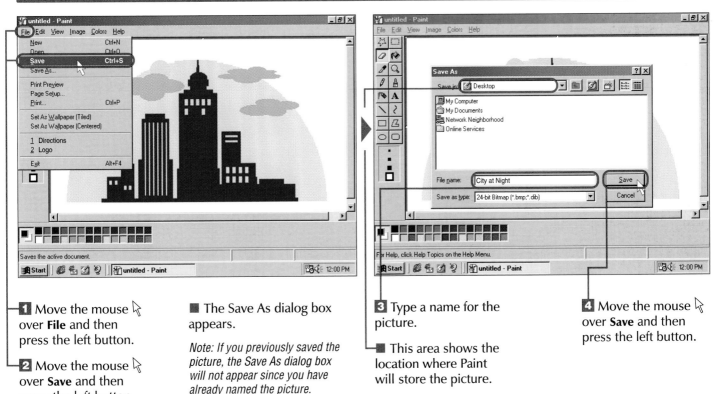

1 Move the mouse ⌖ over **File** and then press the left button.

2 Move the mouse ⌖ over **Save** and then press the left button.

■ The Save As dialog box appears.

Note: If you previously saved the picture, the Save As dialog box will not appear since you have already named the picture.

3 Type a name for the picture.

■ This area shows the location where Paint will store the picture.

4 Move the mouse ⌖ over **Save** and then press the left button.

You can open a saved picture and display the picture on your screen. This allows you to view and make changes to the picture.

OPEN A PICTURE

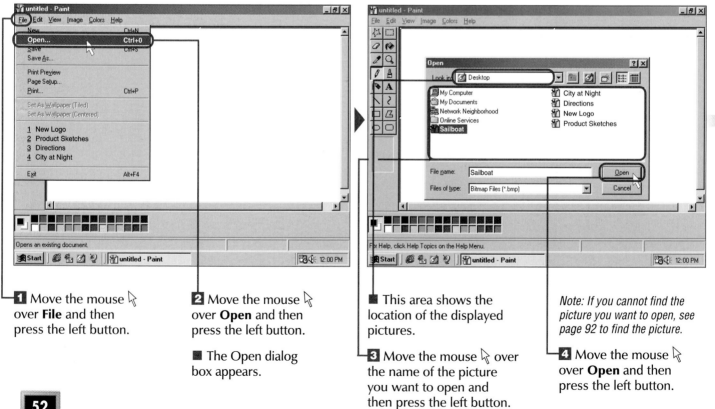

1 Move the mouse over **File** and then press the left button.

2 Move the mouse over **Open** and then press the left button.

■ The Open dialog box appears.

■ This area shows the location of the displayed pictures.

3 Move the mouse over the name of the picture you want to open and then press the left button.

Note: If you cannot find the picture you want to open, see page 92 to find the picture.

4 Move the mouse over **Open** and then press the left button.

Can I work with two pictures open at the same time?

Paint only lets you work with one picture at a time. If you are currently working with a picture, save the picture before opening another. For information on saving a picture, see page 51.

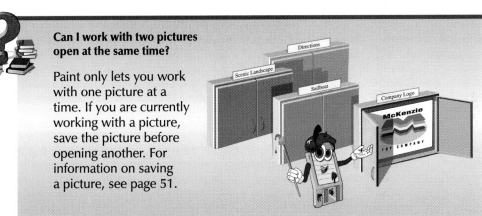

see page 51.

QUICKLY OPEN A PICTURE

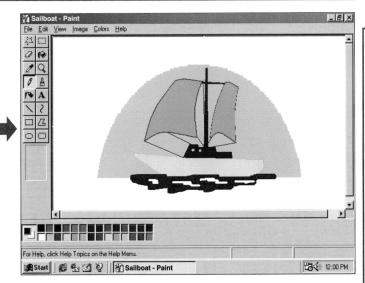

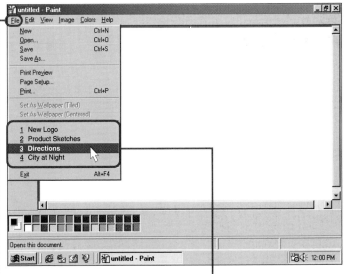

■ Paint opens the picture and displays it on your screen. You can now review and make changes to the picture.

The File menu displays the names of the last four pictures you opened.

1 To quickly open a picture, move the mouse ₭ over **File** and then press the left button.

2 Move the mouse ₭ over the name of the picture you want to open and then press the left button.

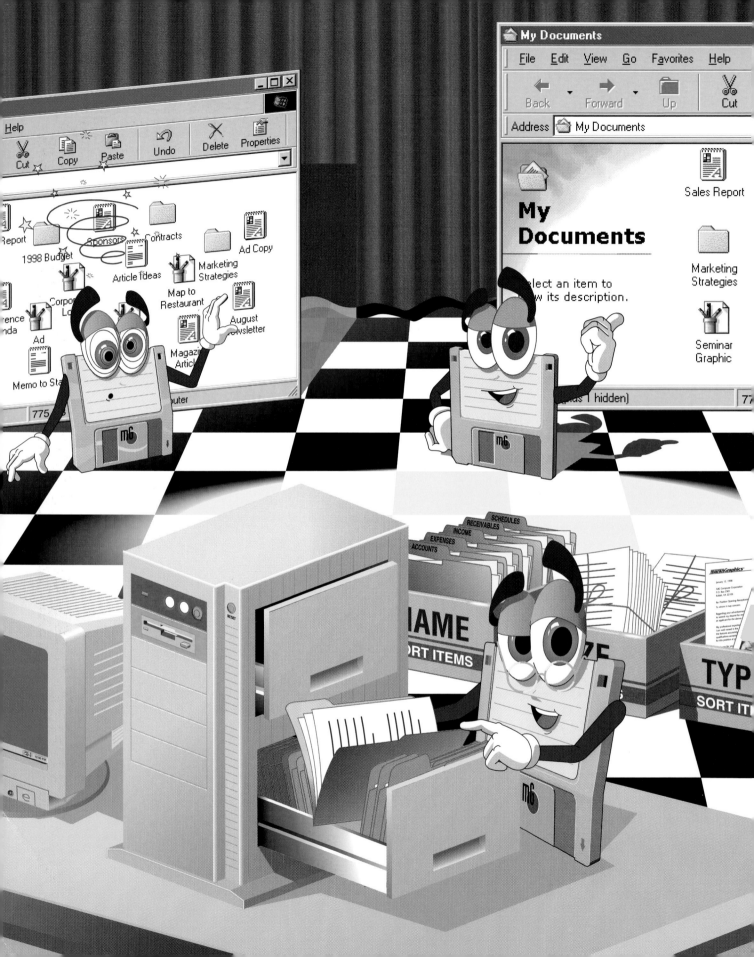

CHAPTER 4

VIEW FILES

Are you looking for a file? Read this chapter to learn how to view the information stored on your computer.

You can easily view the folders and files stored on your computer.

Like a filing cabinet, your computer uses folders to organize information.

VIEW CONTENTS OF YOUR COMPUTER

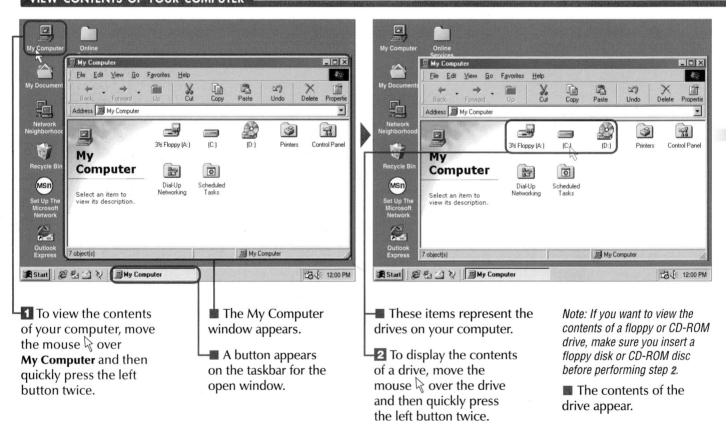

1 To view the contents of your computer, move the mouse � over **My Computer** and then quickly press the left button twice.

■ The My Computer window appears.

■ A button appears on the taskbar for the open window.

■ These items represent the drives on your computer.

2 To display the contents of a drive, move the mouse � over the drive and then quickly press the left button twice.

Note: If you want to view the contents of a floppy or CD-ROM drive, make sure you insert a floppy disk or CD-ROM disc before performing step 2.

■ The contents of the drive appear.

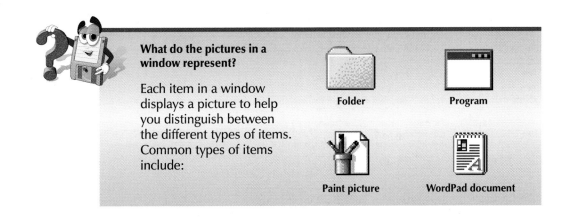

What do the pictures in a window represent?

Each item in a window displays a picture to help you distinguish between the different types of items. Common types of items include:

Folder

Program

Paint picture

WordPad document

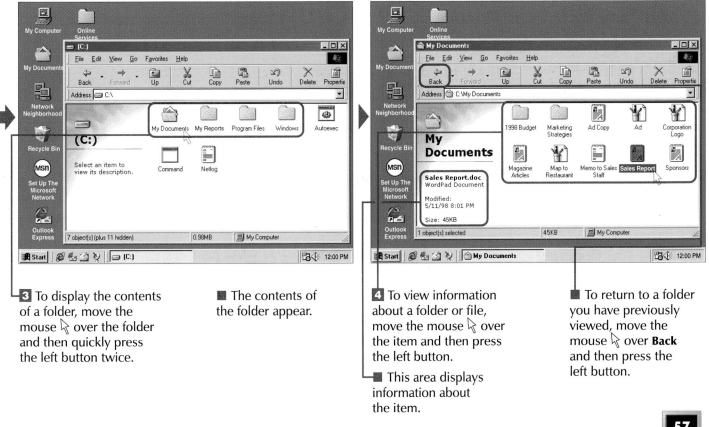

3 To display the contents of a folder, move the mouse Ⓚ over the folder and then quickly press the left button twice.

■ The contents of the folder appear.

4 To view information about a folder or file, move the mouse Ⓚ over the item and then press the left button.

■ This area displays information about the item.

■ To return to a folder you have previously viewed, move the mouse Ⓚ over **Back** and then press the left button.

You can change the appearance of items in a window. Items can appear as large icons, small icons or in a list. You can also display details about each item.

An icon is a picture that represents an item such as a file, folder or program.

CHANGE APPEARANCE OF ITEMS

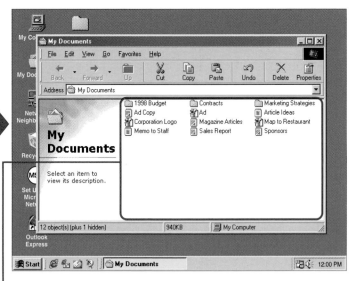

■ When you first start using Windows, items are displayed as large icons.

1 To change the appearance of items, move the mouse ⌖ over **View** and then press the left button.

■ A bullet (•) appears beside the way the items are currently displayed.

2 Move the mouse ⌖ over the way you want to display the items and then press the left button.

SMALL ICONS

■ The items are displayed as small icons.

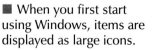

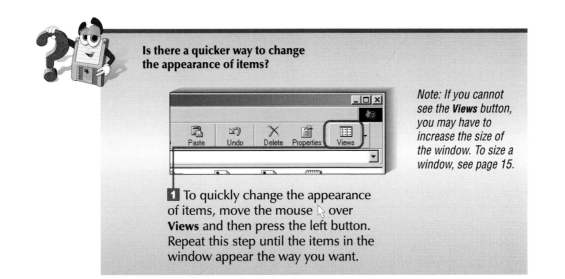

Is there a quicker way to change the appearance of items?

*Note: If you cannot see the **Views** button, you may have to increase the size of the window. To size a window, see page 15.*

1 To quickly change the appearance of items, move the mouse over **Views** and then press the left button. Repeat this step until the items in the window appear the way you want.

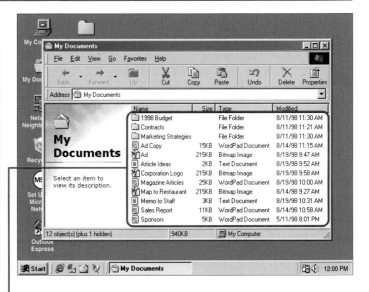

LIST

■ The items are displayed as small icons in a list.

DETAILS

■ Information about each item is displayed, such as the name, size and type of item.

You can sort the items displayed in a window. This can help you find files and folders more easily.

SORT ITEMS

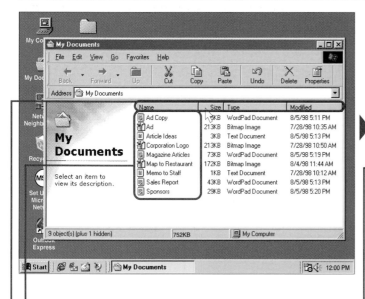

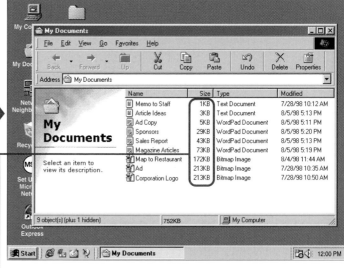

■ When you first start using Windows, items are sorted alphabetically by name.

1 Move the mouse ⊹ over the heading for the column you want to use to sort the items and then press the left button.

Note: If the headings are not displayed, perform steps 1 and 2 on page 58, selecting Details in step 2.

■ To sort the items in reverse order, move the mouse ⊹ over the heading again and then press the left button.

SORT BY SIZE

■ The items are sorted by size from smallest to largest.

60

How does Windows measure the size of files?

The size of each file is measured in kilobytes (KB). An average letter created in WordPad is approximately 5 KB.

SORT BY TYPE

■ The items are sorted alphabetically by type.

SORT BY DATE

■ The items are sorted by the date they were last saved.

ARRANGE ITEMS AUTOMATICALLY

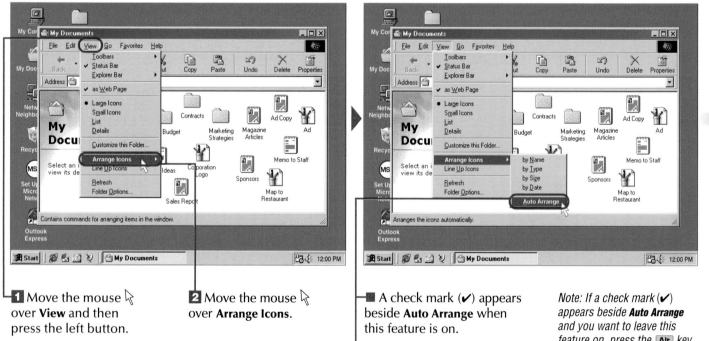

1 Move the mouse over **View** and then press the left button.

2 Move the mouse over **Arrange Icons**.

■ A check mark (✔) appears beside **Auto Arrange** when this feature is on.

3 To turn this feature on, move the mouse over **Auto Arrange** and then press the left button.

Note: If a check mark (✔) appears beside Auto Arrange and you want to leave this feature on, press the Alt key to close the menu.

Why is the Auto Arrange feature not available?

The Auto Arrange feature is not available when items appear in the List or Details view. For information on changing the appearance of items, see page 58.

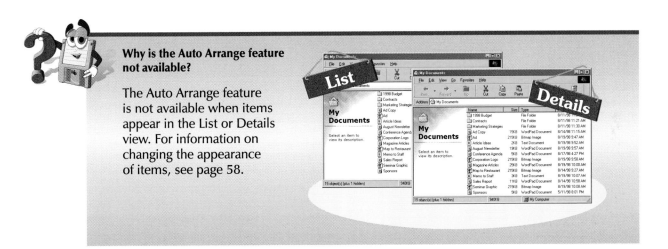

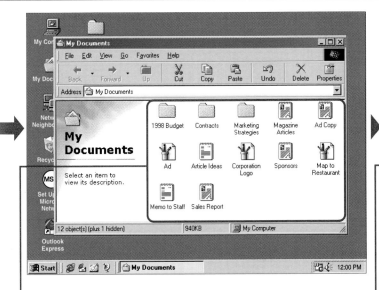

■ The items are automatically arranged in the window.

■ To turn off the Auto Arrange feature, repeat steps 1 to 3.

■ When you change the size of a window and the Auto Arrange feature is on, Windows automatically rearranges the items to fit the new window size.

Note: To size a window, see page 15.

> Windows Explorer shows the location of every folder and file on your computer.

USING WINDOWS EXPLORER

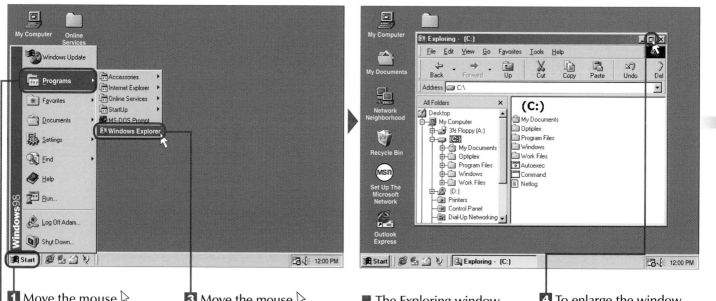

1 Move the mouse ⬚ over **Start** and then press the left button.

2 Move the mouse ⬚ over **Programs**.

3 Move the mouse ⬚ over **Windows Explorer** and then press the left button.

■ The Exploring window appears.

4 To enlarge the window to fill your screen, move the mouse ⬚ over ▢ and then press the left button.

How can I work with files in Windows Explorer?

You can work with files in Windows Explorer as you would work with files in a My Computer window. For example, you can move, rename and delete files in Windows Explorer.

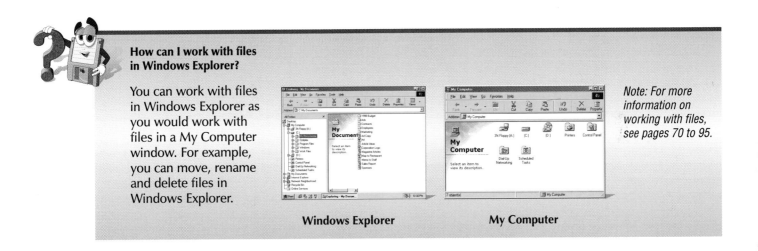

Windows Explorer

My Computer

Note: For more information on working with files, see pages 70 to 95.

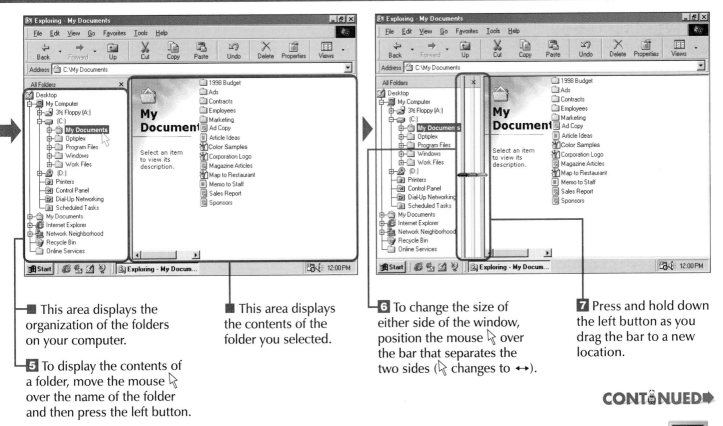

■ This area displays the organization of the folders on your computer.

5 To display the contents of a folder, move the mouse ⬚ over the name of the folder and then press the left button.

■ This area displays the contents of the folder you selected.

6 To change the size of either side of the window, position the mouse ⬚ over the bar that separates the two sides (⬚ changes to ↔).

7 Press and hold down the left button as you drag the bar to a new location.

CONTINUED➡

DISPLAY HIDDEN FOLDERS

You can display hidden folders to view more of the contents of your computer.

1 To display the hidden folders within a folder, move the mouse ⟍ over the plus sign (⊞) beside the folder and then press the left button.

■ The hidden folders appear.

■ The plus sign (⊞) beside the folder changes to a minus sign (⊟). This indicates that all the folders within the folder are now displayed.

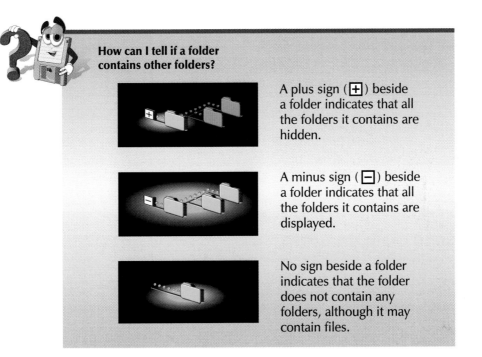

How can I tell if a folder contains other folders?

A plus sign (⊞) beside a folder indicates that all the folders it contains are hidden.

A minus sign (⊟) beside a folder indicates that all the folders it contains are displayed.

No sign beside a folder indicates that the folder does not contain any folders, although it may contain files.

HIDE FOLDERS

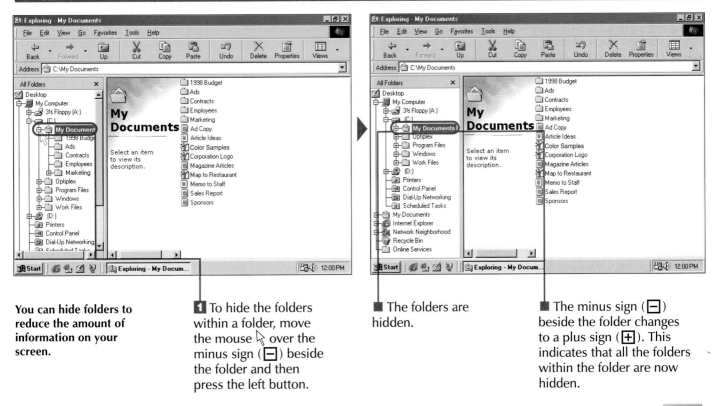

You can hide folders to reduce the amount of information on your screen.

■1 To hide the folders within a folder, move the mouse ⤵ over the minus sign (⊟) beside the folder and then press the left button.

■ The folders are hidden.

■ The minus sign (⊟) beside the folder changes to a plus sign (⊞). This indicates that all the folders within the folder are now hidden.

CHAPTER 5

WORK WITH FILES

Are you wondering how to open, move and copy your files? Would you like to print your files? This chapter shows you how.

You can open a file to display its contents on your screen. This lets you review and make changes to the file.

OPEN A FILE

1 Move the mouse ⍅ over the file you want to open and then quickly press the left button twice.

■ The file opens. You can review and make changes to the file.

2 When you finish working with the file, move the mouse ⍅ over ☒ and then press the left button.

OPEN A RECENTLY USED FILE

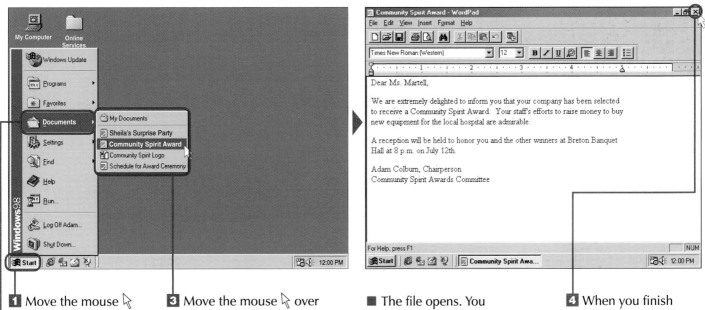

1 Move the mouse over **Start** and then press the left button.

2 Move the mouse over **Documents**.

3 Move the mouse over the file you want to open and then press the left button.

*Note: The My Documents folder stores many documents you have created. To open the folder, move the mouse over **My Documents** and then press the left button.*

■ The file opens. You can review and make changes to the file.

4 When you finish working with the file, move the mouse over ☒ and then press the left button.

Before working with files, you must first select the files you want to work with. Selected files appear highlighted on your screen.

You can select folders the same way you select files. Selecting a folder will select all the files in the folder.

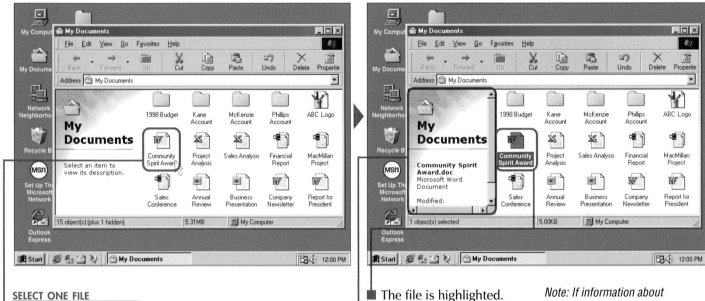

SELECT ONE FILE

1 Move the mouse ⤢ over the file you want to select and then press the left button.

■ The file is highlighted.

■ This area displays information about the file.

Note: If information about the file does not appear, you may need to change to the Web style. To change to the Web style, see page 118.

How do I deselect files?

To deselect all of the files in a window, move the mouse ⌖ over a blank area in the window and then press the left button.

To deselect one file from a group of selected files, press and hold down the `Ctrl` key while you move the mouse ⌖ over the file you want to deselect and then press the left button.

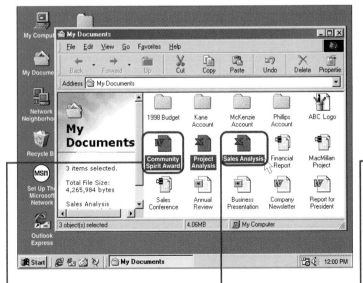

SELECT A GROUP OF FILES

1 Move the mouse ⌖ over the first file you want to select and then press the left button.

2 Press and hold down the `Shift` key.

3 Still holding down the `Shift` key, move the mouse ⌖ over the last file you want to select and then press the left button.

SELECT RANDOM FILES

1 Move the mouse ⌖ over a file you want to select and then press the left button.

2 Press and hold down the `Ctrl` key.

3 Still holding down the `Ctrl` key, move the mouse ⌖ over each file you want to select and then press the left button.

You can give a file a new name to better describe the contents of the file. This can make the file easier to find.

RENAME A FILE

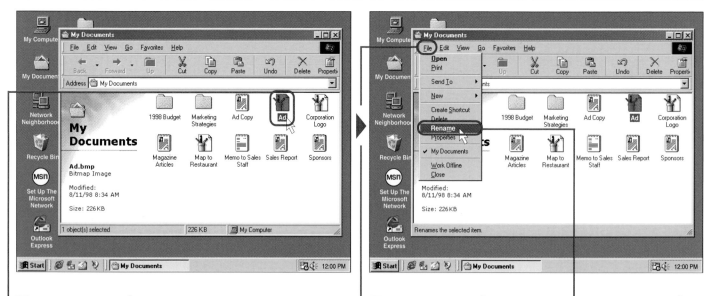

1 Move the mouse ℝ over the file you want to rename and then press the left button.

2 Move the mouse ℝ over **File** and then press the left button.

3 Move the mouse ℝ over **Rename** and then press the left button.

Can I rename a folder?

You should only rename folders that you have created. To rename a folder, perform the steps below, selecting the folder you want to rename in step **1**.

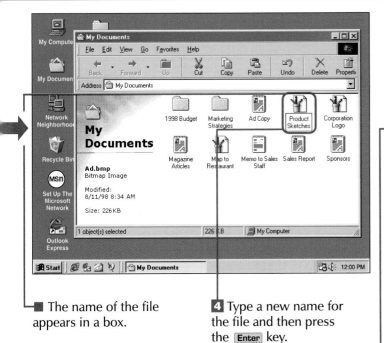

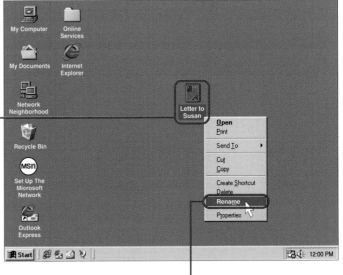

■ The name of the file appears in a box.

4 Type a new name for the file and then press the Enter key.

*Note: You can use up to 255 characters to name a file. The name cannot contain the \ /: * ? " < > or | characters.*

You can easily rename a file on your desktop.

1 Move the mouse ⬚ over the file and then press the **right** button. A menu appears.

2 Move the mouse ⬚ over **Rename** and then press the left button.

3 Type a new name and then press the Enter key.

You can create a new folder to help you better organize the information stored on your computer. Creating a folder is like placing a new folder in a filing cabinet.

CREATE A NEW FOLDER

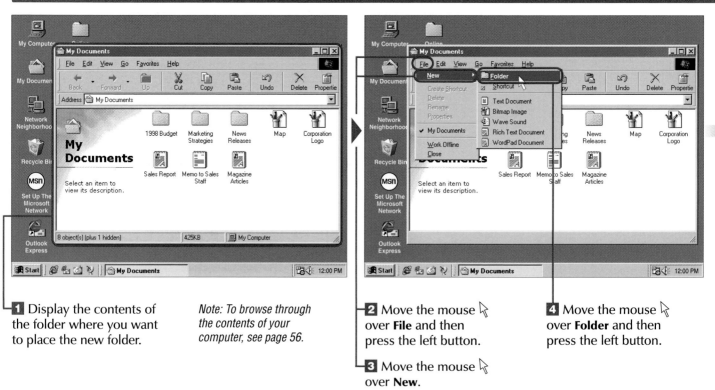

1 Display the contents of the folder where you want to place the new folder.

Note: To browse through the contents of your computer, see page 56.

2 Move the mouse over **File** and then press the left button.

3 Move the mouse over **New**.

4 Move the mouse over **Folder** and then press the left button.

How can creating new folders help me organize the information on my computer?

You can create as many new folders as you need to develop a filing system that works for you. You can then organize your files by moving them to the new folders. To move files, see page 78.

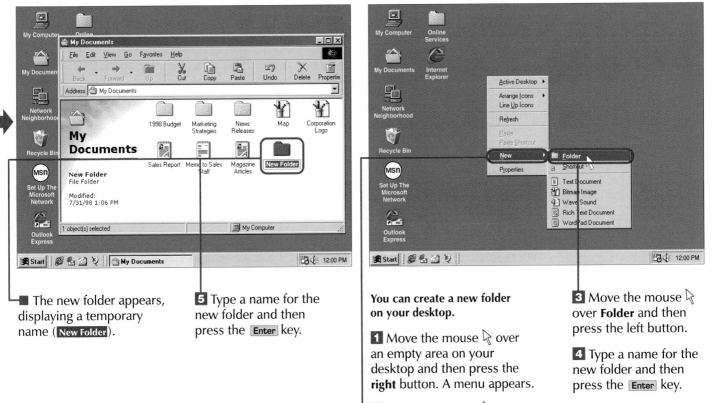

■ The new folder appears, displaying a temporary name (New Folder).

5 Type a name for the new folder and then press the Enter key.

You can create a new folder on your desktop.

1 Move the mouse ⟨ over an empty area on your desktop and then press the **right** button. A menu appears.

2 Move the mouse ⟨ over **New**.

3 Move the mouse ⟨ over **Folder** and then press the left button.

4 Type a name for the new folder and then press the Enter key.

You can organize the files stored on your computer by moving or copying them to new locations.

Organizing files on your computer is similar to organizing files in a filing cabinet.

MOVE FILES

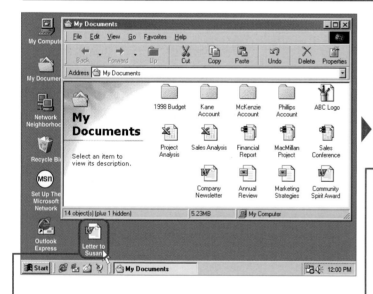

1 Position the mouse ⍾ over the file you want to move.

■ To move more than one file, select all the files you want to move. Then position the mouse ⍾ over one of the files.

Note: To select multiple files, see page 73.

2 Press and hold down the left button as you drag the file to a new location on your computer.

What is the difference between moving and copying a file?

Move a File

When you move a file, you place the file in a new location on your computer.

Copy a File

When you copy a file, you make an exact copy of the file and then place the copy in a new location. This lets you store the file in two locations.

COPY FILES

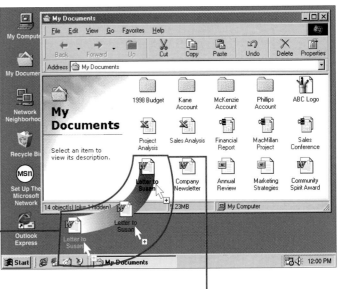

The file moves to the new location.

Note: You can move folders the same way you move files. When you move a folder, all the files in the folder also move.

■ Position the mouse over the file you want to copy.

■ Press and hold down the **Ctrl** key.

■ Still holding down the **Ctrl** key, press and hold down the left button as you drag the file to a new location.

You can make an exact copy of a file and then place the copy on a floppy disk. This is useful if you want to give a colleague a copy of the file.

COPY A FILE TO A FLOPPY DISK

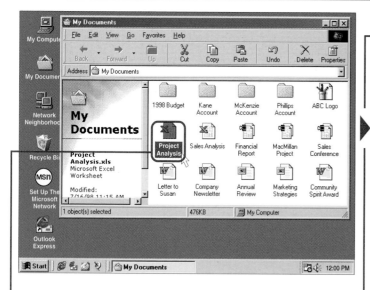

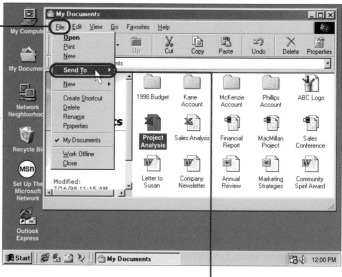

1 Insert a floppy disk into the floppy drive.

2 Move the mouse over the file you want to copy and then press the left button.

■ To copy more than one file, select all the files you want to copy.

Note: To select multiple files, see page 73.

3 Move the mouse over **File** and then press the left button.

4 Move the mouse over **Send To**.

How can I protect the information on my floppy disks?

You should keep floppy disks away from magnets, which can damage the information stored on the disks. Also be careful not to spill liquids, such as coffee or soda, on the disks.

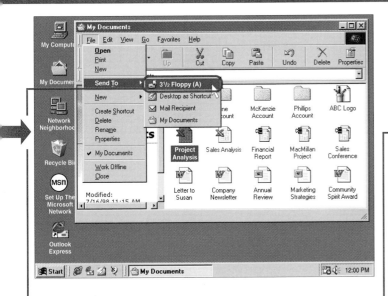

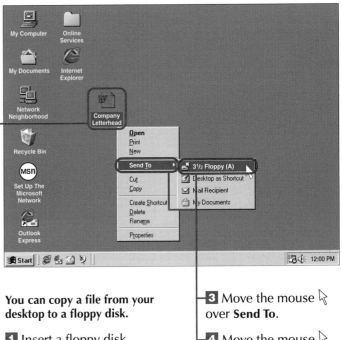

5 Move the mouse ⃗ over the drive that contains the floppy disk you want to receive a copy of the file and then press the left button.

■ Windows places a copy of the file on the floppy disk.

Note: You can copy a folder the same way you copy a file. When you copy a folder, all the files in the folder are also copied.

You can copy a file from your desktop to a floppy disk.

1 Insert a floppy disk into the floppy drive.

2 Move the mouse ⃗ over the file you want to copy and then press the **right** button. A menu appears.

3 Move the mouse ⃗ over **Send To**.

4 Move the mouse ⃗ over the drive that contains the floppy disk and then press the left button.

You can delete a file you no longer need.

Before you delete any files you have created, consider the value of your work. Do not delete a file unless you are certain you no longer need the file.

DELETE A FILE

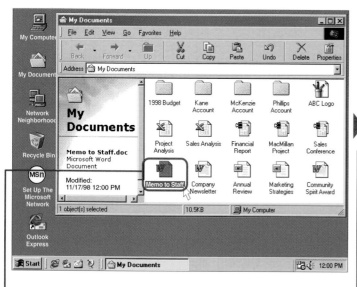

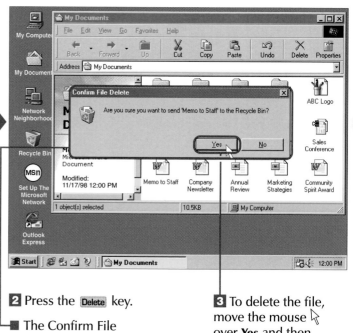

1 Move the mouse over the file you want to delete and then press the left button.

■ To delete more than one file, select the files.

Note: To select multiple files, see page 73.

2 Press the Delete key.

■ The Confirm File Delete dialog box appears.

3 To delete the file, move the mouse over **Yes** and then press the left button.

Can I delete any file on my computer?

Make sure you only delete files that you have created. Do not delete any files that Windows or other programs require to operate.

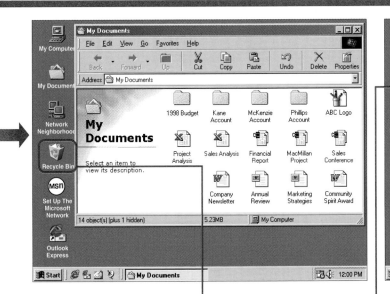

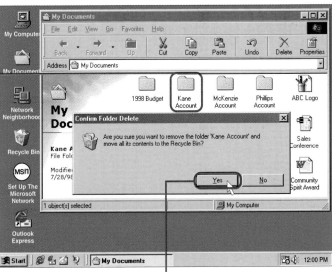

■ The file disappears.

■ Windows places the file in the Recycle Bin.

Note: To restore a file from the Recycle Bin, see page 84.

You can delete a folder and all the files it contains.

◀1 Move the mouse ⃗ over the folder you want to delete and then press the left button.

2 Press the Delete key.

■ The Confirm Folder Delete dialog box appears.

3 To delete the folder, move the mouse ⃗ over **Yes** and then press the left button.

The Recycle Bin stores all the files you have deleted. You can easily restore any of these files.

RESTORE A DELETED FILE

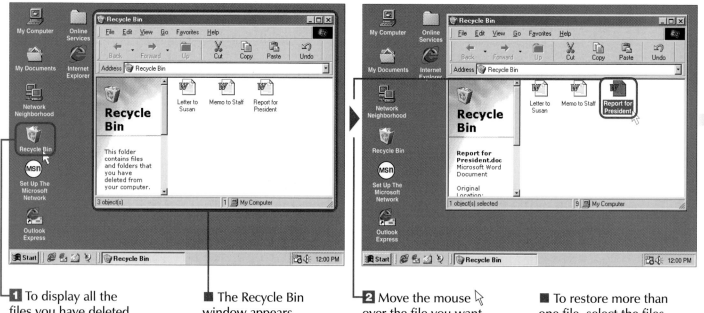

■1 To display all the files you have deleted, move the mouse ⟍ over **Recycle Bin** and then quickly press the left button twice.

■ The Recycle Bin window appears, displaying all the files you have deleted.

■2 Move the mouse ⟍ over the file you want to restore and then press the left button.

■ To restore more than one file, select the files.

Note: To select multiple files, see page 73.

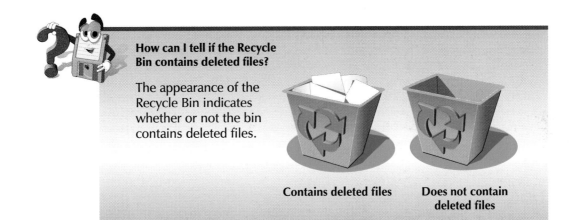

How can I tell if the Recycle Bin contains deleted files?

The appearance of the Recycle Bin indicates whether or not the bin contains deleted files.

Contains deleted files

Does not contain deleted files

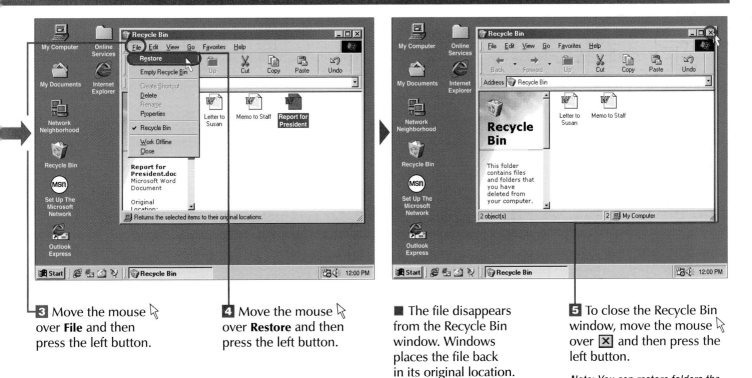

3 Move the mouse ⇗ over **File** and then press the left button.

4 Move the mouse ⇗ over **Restore** and then press the left button.

■ The file disappears from the Recycle Bin window. Windows places the file back in its original location.

5 To close the Recycle Bin window, move the mouse ⇗ over ⊠ and then press the left button.

Note: You can restore folders the same way you restore files. When you restore a folder, all the files in the folder are also restored.

EMPTY THE RECYCLE BIN

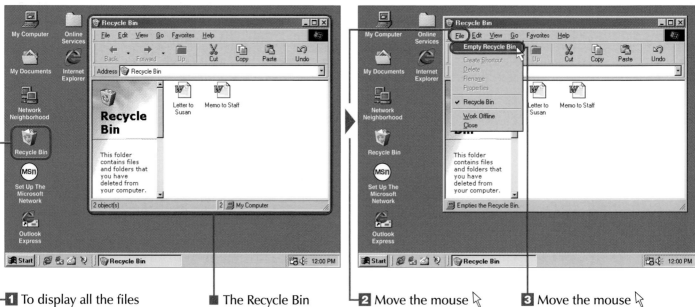

> You can create more free space on your computer by permanently removing all the files from the Recycle Bin.

1 To display all the files you have deleted, move the mouse ⟶ over **Recycle Bin** and then quickly press the left button twice.

■ The Recycle Bin window appears, displaying all the files you have deleted.

2 Move the mouse ⟶ over **File** and then press the left button.

3 Move the mouse ⟶ over **Empty Recycle Bin** and then press the left button.

What if the Recycle Bin contains a file I may need?

Before emptying the Recycle Bin, make sure it does not contain files you may need in the future. To restore a file you may need, see page 84. Once you empty the Recycle Bin, the files are permanently removed from your computer and cannot be restored.

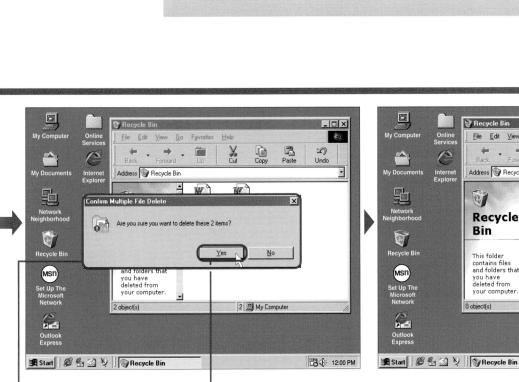

■ The Confirm Multiple File Delete dialog box appears.

4 To permanently delete all the files, move the mouse ⓀȘ over **Yes** and then press the left button.

■ All the files are permanently deleted from your computer.

5 To close the Recycle Bin window, move the mouse ⓀȘ over ✕ and then press the left button.

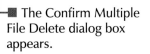

You can produce a paper copy of a file stored on your computer. Before printing, make sure your printer is turned on and contains paper.

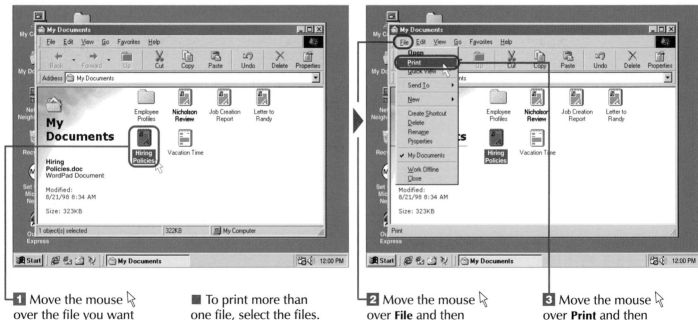

1 Move the mouse over the file you want to print and then press the left button.

■ To print more than one file, select the files.

Note: To select multiple files, see page 73.

2 Move the mouse over **File** and then press the left button.

3 Move the mouse over **Print** and then press the left button.

What types of printers can I use to print my files?

Windows works with many types of printers. There are two common types of printers.

Ink-jet

An ink-jet printer produces documents that are suitable for routine business and personal use.

Laser

A laser printer is faster and produces higher-quality documents than an ink-jet printer, but is more expensive.

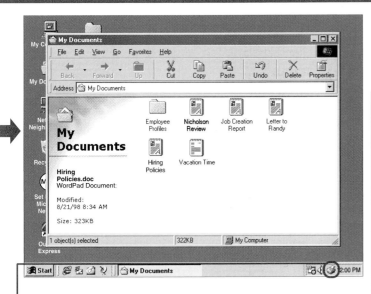

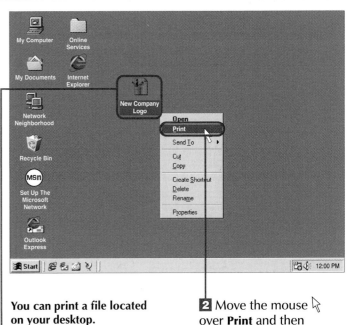

■ When you print a file, the printer icon (🖨) appears in this area. The icon disappears when the file has finished printing.

You can print a file located on your desktop.

1 Move the mouse ⬚ over the file you want to print and then press the **right** button. A menu appears.

2 Move the mouse ⬚ over **Print** and then press the left button.

You can view information about the files you sent to the printer.

VIEW FILES SENT TO THE PRINTER

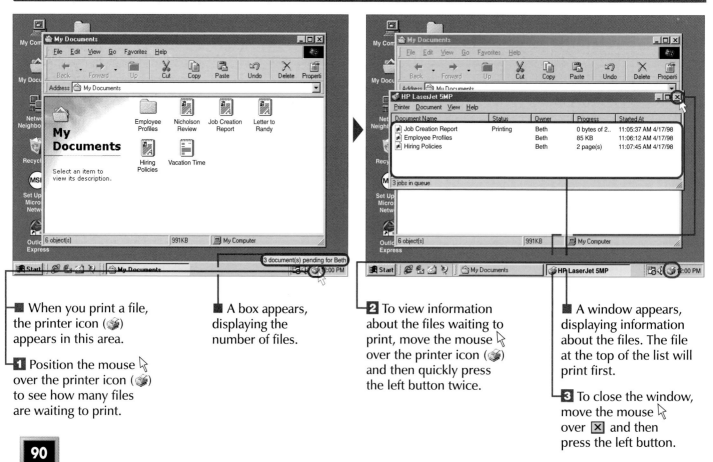

◼ When you print a file, the printer icon (🖨) appears in this area.

1 Position the mouse ⬚ over the printer icon (🖨) to see how many files are waiting to print.

◼ A box appears, displaying the number of files.

2 To view information about the files waiting to print, move the mouse ⬚ over the printer icon (🖨) and then quickly press the left button twice.

◼ A window appears, displaying information about the files. The file at the top of the list will print first.

3 To close the window, move the mouse ⬚ over ☒ and then press the left button.

You can stop a file from printing. This is useful if you want to make last-minute changes to the file.

CANCEL PRINTING

1 Move the mouse ⬚ over the printer icon (🖨) and then quickly press the left button twice.

■ A window appears, displaying information about the files waiting to print.

2 Move the mouse ⬚ over the file you no longer want to print and then press the left button.

3 Press the Delete key and the file disappears from the list.

4 To close the window, move the mouse ⬚ over ⊠ and then press the left button.

If you cannot remember the exact name or location of a file you want to work with, you can have Windows search for the file.

Find: Sales Meeting

FIND A FILE

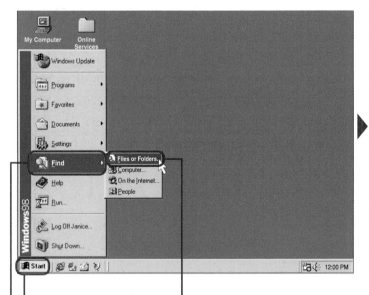

1 Move the mouse ⟍ over **Start** and then press the left button.

2 Move the mouse ⟍ over **Find**.

3 Move the mouse ⟍ over **Files or Folders** and then press the left button.

■ The Find window appears.

4 To specify the name of the file you want to find, move the mouse I over this area and then press the left button. Then type all or part of the name.

5 To specify a word or phrase within the file you want to find, move the mouse I over this area and then press the left button. Then type the word or phrase.

Can I search for a file if I only know part of the file name?

If you search for part of a file name, Windows will find all the files with names that contain the word you specified. For example, searching for the word "report" will find every file or folder with a name containing the word "report".

Find:
Report

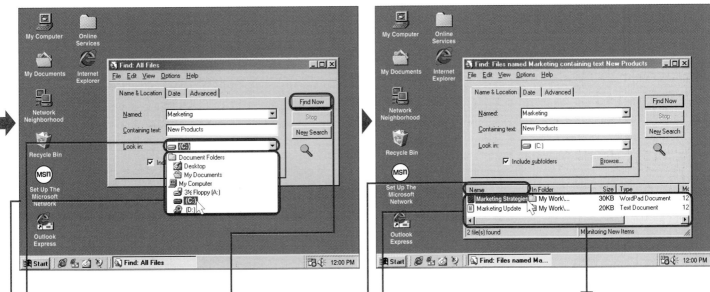

■6 To specify where you want Windows to search for the file, move the mouse ▷ over ▼ in this area and then press the left button.

■7 Move the mouse ▷ over the location you want to search and then press the left button.

■8 To start the search, move the mouse ▷ over **Find Now** and then press the left button.

■ This area displays the names of the files Windows found and information about each file.

■ If Windows found several files, move the mouse ▷ over the **Name** heading to sort the files alphabetically and then press the left button.

■9 To open a file, move the mouse ▷ over the name of the file and then quickly press the left button twice.

You can add a shortcut to the desktop to provide a quick way of opening a file you use regularly.

ADD A SHORTCUT TO THE DESKTOP

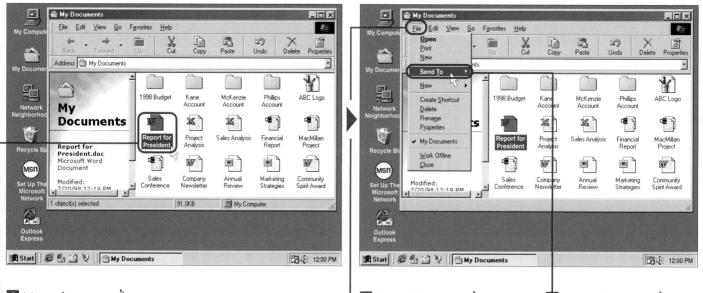

1 Move the mouse ⬉ over the file you want to create a shortcut to and then press the left button.

2 Move the mouse ⬉ over **File** and then press the left button.

3 Move the mouse ⬉ over **Send To**.

How do I rename or delete a shortcut?

You can rename or delete a shortcut the same way you would rename or delete any file. Renaming or deleting a shortcut does not affect the original file. For information on renaming a file, see page 74. For information on deleting a file, see page 82.

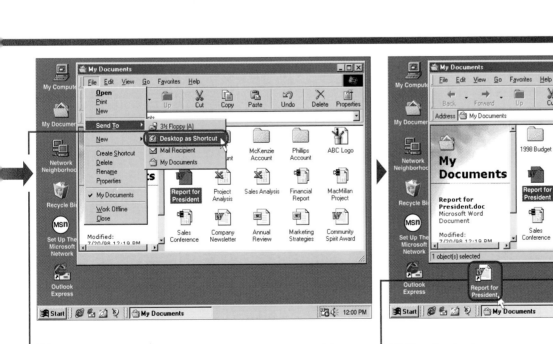

■4 Move the mouse ⟍ over **Desktop as Shortcut** or **Desktop (create shortcut)** and then press the left button.

Note: The name of the command depends on the version of Windows 98 you are using.

■ The shortcut appears on the desktop.

■ You can tell the difference between the original file and the shortcut because the shortcut displays an arrow (▟).

■ To open the file, move the mouse ⟍ over the shortcut and then quickly press the left button twice.

CHAPTER 6

CUSTOMIZE WINDOWS

Do you want to customize Windows settings? In this chapter you will learn how to move and size the taskbar, change the patterns and colors on your screen and much more.

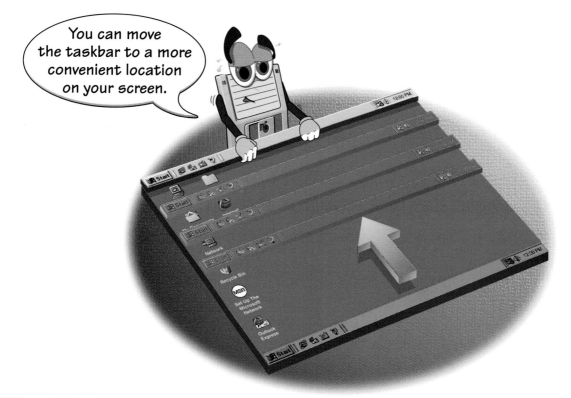

MOVE THE TASKBAR

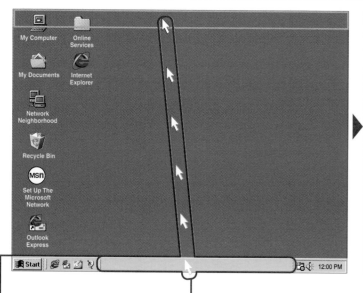

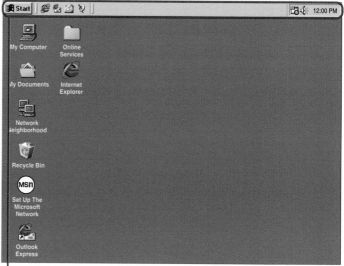

1 Position the mouse over a blank area on the taskbar.

2 Press and hold down the left button as you drag the taskbar to a new location on your screen.

■ The taskbar moves to the new location.

Note: You can move the taskbar to the top, bottom, left or right edge of your screen.

You can change the size of the taskbar so it can display more information.

SIZE THE TASKBAR

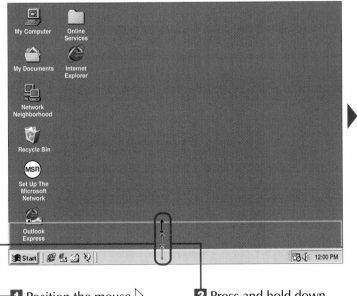

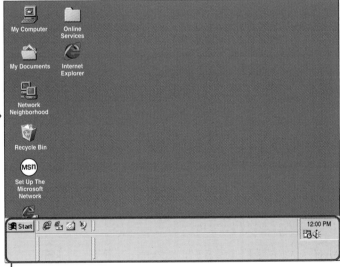

1 Position the mouse ⌖ over the edge of the taskbar (⌖ changes to ↕).

2 Press and hold down the left button as you drag the mouse ↕ until the taskbar displays the size you want.

■ The taskbar displays the new size.

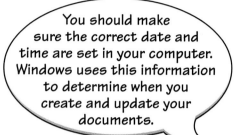

You should make sure the correct date and time are set in your computer. Windows uses this information to determine when you create and update your documents.

CHANGE THE DATE AND TIME

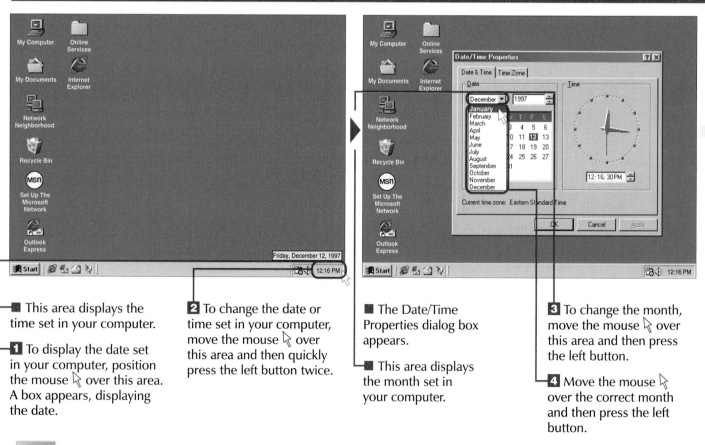

■ This area displays the time set in your computer.

1 To display the date set in your computer, position the mouse ↖ over this area. A box appears, displaying the date.

2 To change the date or time set in your computer, move the mouse ↖ over this area and then quickly press the left button twice.

■ The Date/Time Properties dialog box appears.

■ This area displays the month set in your computer.

3 To change the month, move the mouse ↖ over this area and then press the left button.

4 Move the mouse ↖ over the correct month and then press the left button.

Will Windows keep track of the date and time even when I turn off my computer?

Your computer has a built-in clock that keeps track of the date and time even when you turn off the computer.

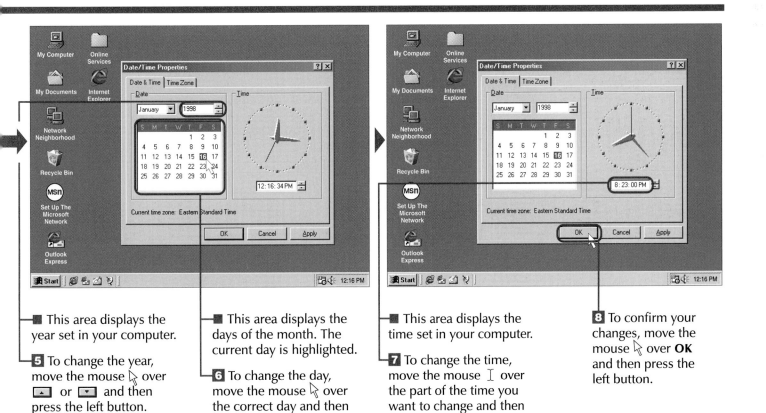

■ This area displays the year set in your computer.

5 To change the year, move the mouse ⍩ over ▄▀ or ▀▼ and then press the left button.

■ This area displays the days of the month. The current day is highlighted.

6 To change the day, move the mouse ⍩ over the correct day and then press the left button.

■ This area displays the time set in your computer.

7 To change the time, move the mouse I over the part of the time you want to change and then quickly press the left button twice. Then type the correct information.

8 To confirm your changes, move the mouse ⍩ over **OK** and then press the left button.

You can decorate your screen by adding wallpaper.

ADD WALLPAPER

1 Move the mouse ⌖ over a blank area on your desktop and then press the **right** button. A menu appears.

2 Move the mouse ⌖ over **Properties** and then press the left button.

■ The Display Properties dialog box appears.

3 Move the mouse ⌖ over the wallpaper you want to use and then press the left button.

4 To select how you want to display the wallpaper, move the mouse ⌖ over this area and then press the left button.

5 Move the mouse ⌖ over an option and then press the left button.

Note: For more information, see the top of page 103.

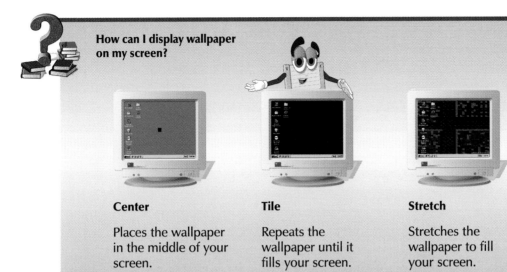

How can I display wallpaper on my screen?

Center

Places the wallpaper in the middle of your screen.

Tile

Repeats the wallpaper until it fills your screen.

Stretch

Stretches the wallpaper to fill your screen.

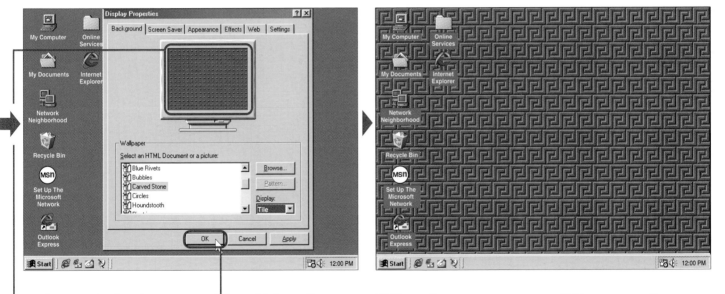

■ This area displays how the wallpaper you selected will look on your screen.

6 To add the wallpaper to your screen, move the mouse ⟍ over **OK** and then press the left button.

■ The wallpaper appears on your screen.

■ To remove wallpaper from your screen, repeat steps **1** to **3**, selecting **(None)** in step **3**. Then perform step **6**.

A screen saver is a moving picture or pattern that appears on the screen when you do not use your computer for a period of time.

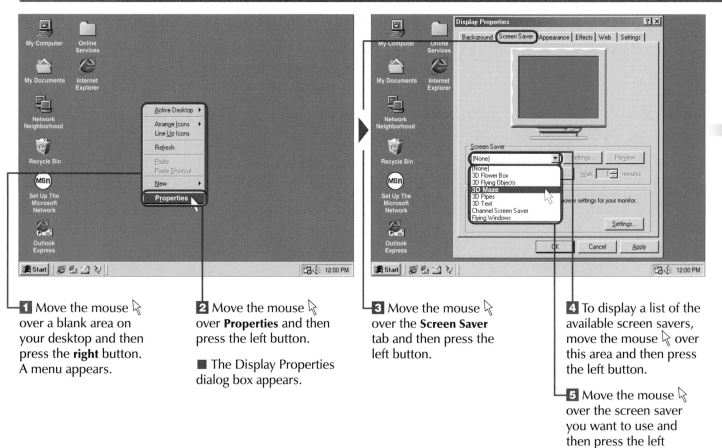

1 Move the mouse ⌖ over a blank area on your desktop and then press the **right** button. A menu appears.

2 Move the mouse ⌖ over **Properties** and then press the left button.

■ The Display Properties dialog box appears.

3 Move the mouse ⌖ over the **Screen Saver** tab and then press the left button.

4 To display a list of the available screen savers, move the mouse ⌖ over this area and then press the left button.

5 Move the mouse ⌖ over the screen saver you want to use and then press the left button.

Do I need to use a screen saver?

Screen savers were originally designed to prevent screen burn, which occurs when an image appears in a fixed position on the screen for a period of time. Today's monitors are better designed to prevent screen burn, but people still use screen savers for their entertainment value.

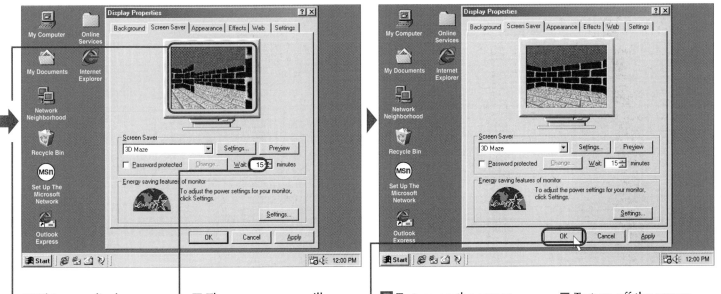

■ This area displays how the screen saver will look on your screen.

■ The screen saver will appear when you do not use your computer for the number of minutes shown in this area.

6 To change the number of minutes, move the mouse I over this area and then quickly press the left button twice. Then type a new number.

7 To turn on the screen saver, move the mouse over **OK** and then press the left button.

■ When the screen saver appears on your screen, you can move the mouse or press a key on your keyboard to remove the screen saver.

■ To turn off the screen saver, repeat steps 1 to 5, selecting **(None)** in step 5. Then perform step 7.

You can change the colors displayed on your screen to personalize and enhance Windows.

CHANGE SCREEN COLORS

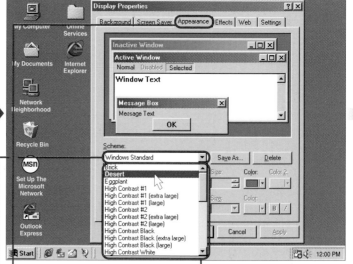

1 Move the mouse ⌖ over a blank area on your desktop and then press the **right** button. A menu appears.

2 Move the mouse ⌖ over **Properties** and then press the left button.

■ The Display Properties dialog box appears.

3 Move the mouse ⌖ over the **Appearance** tab and then press the left button.

4 To display a list of the available color schemes, move the mouse ⌖ over this area and then press the left button.

5 Move the mouse ⌖ over the color scheme you want to use and then press the left button.

What is the difference between the High Contrast, high color and VGA color schemes?

Note: For information on changing the number of colors your computer displays, see page 112.

High Contrast schemes are designed for people with vision impairments.

High color schemes are designed for computers displaying more than 256 colors.

VGA schemes are designed for computers limited to 16 colors.

■ This area displays how your screen will look with the color scheme you selected.

6 To add the color scheme, move the mouse ⬚ over **OK** and then press the left button.

■ Your screen displays the color scheme you selected.

■ To return to the original color scheme, perform steps 1 to 6, selecting **Windows Standard** in step 5.

Before you can use a desktop theme, you may need to add the Desktop Themes component to your computer. To add a Windows component, see page 158.

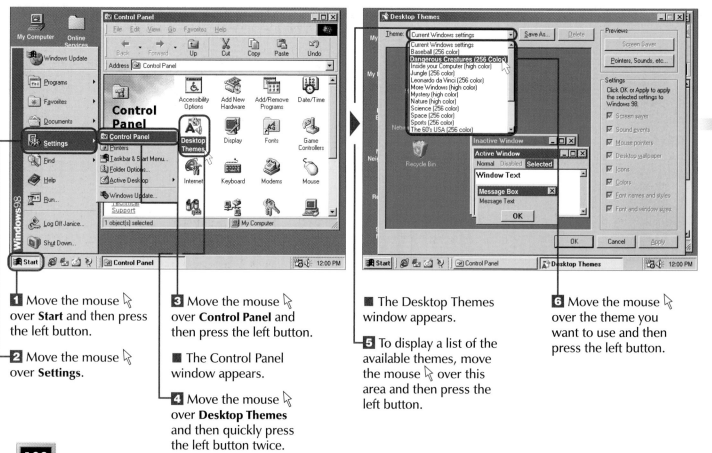

1 Move the mouse ⫛ over **Start** and then press the left button.

2 Move the mouse ⫛ over **Settings**.

3 Move the mouse ⫛ over **Control Panel** and then press the left button.

■ The Control Panel window appears.

4 Move the mouse ⫛ over **Desktop Themes** and then quickly press the left button twice.

■ The Desktop Themes window appears.

5 To display a list of the available themes, move the mouse ⫛ over this area and then press the left button.

6 Move the mouse ⫛ over the theme you want to use and then press the left button.

If I add a desktop theme, what items will change?

A desktop theme will change the colors, sounds, wallpaper, screen saver, mouse pointers and icons on your computer.

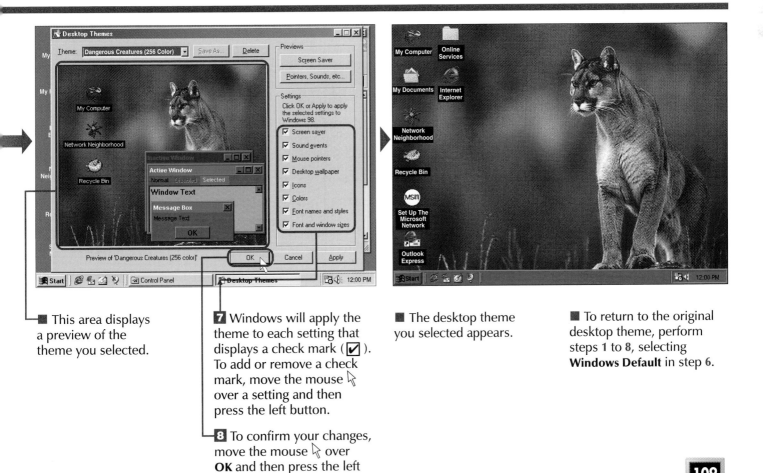

■ This area displays a preview of the theme you selected.

7 Windows will apply the theme to each setting that displays a check mark (☑). To add or remove a check mark, move the mouse ⌖ over a setting and then press the left button.

8 To confirm your changes, move the mouse ⌖ over **OK** and then press the left button.

■ The desktop theme you selected appears.

■ To return to the original desktop theme, perform steps **1** to **8**, selecting **Windows Default** in step **6**.

You can change the amount of information that can fit on your screen.

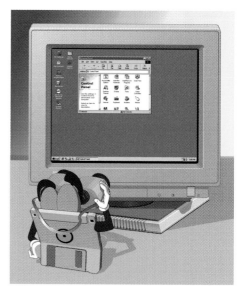

Lower resolutions display larger images on the screen. This lets you see information more clearly.

Higher resolutions display smaller images on the screen. This lets you display more information at once.

CHANGE SCREEN RESOLUTION

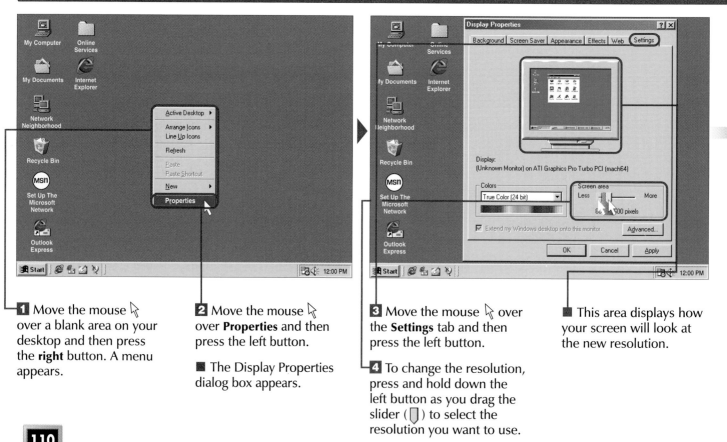

1 Move the mouse ⌖ over a blank area on your desktop and then press the **right** button. A menu appears.

2 Move the mouse ⌖ over **Properties** and then press the left button.

■ The Display Properties dialog box appears.

3 Move the mouse ⌖ over the **Settings** tab and then press the left button.

4 To change the resolution, press and hold down the left button as you drag the slider (▯) to select the resolution you want to use.

■ This area displays how your screen will look at the new resolution.

Can I change my screen resolution?

Your monitor and video card determine if you can change your screen resolution.

5 To confirm the change, move the mouse ⍟ over **OK** and then press the left button.

■ A dialog box appears.

6 To change the resolution, move the mouse ⍟ over **OK** and then press the left button.

■ Windows resizes the information on your screen.

■ The Monitor Settings dialog box appears, asking if you want to keep the setting.

7 To keep the setting, move the mouse ⍟ over **Yes** and then press the left button.

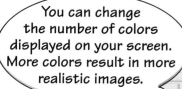

You can change the number of colors displayed on your screen. More colors result in more realistic images.

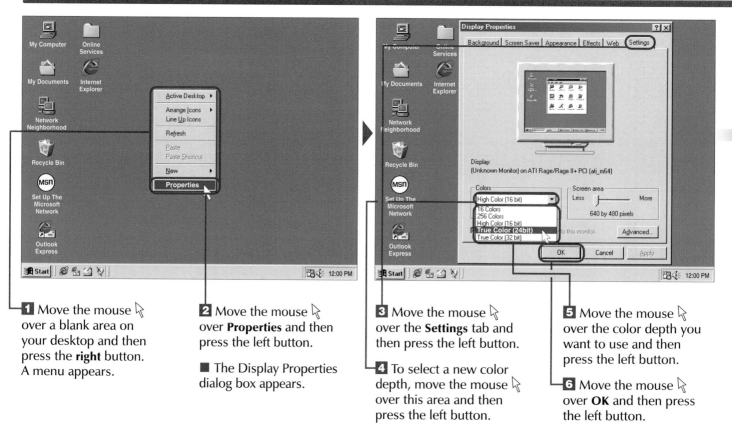

Your monitor and video card determine the maximum number of colors your screen can display.

CHANGE COLOR DEPTH

1 Move the mouse ⌖ over a blank area on your desktop and then press the **right** button. A menu appears.

2 Move the mouse ⌖ over **Properties** and then press the left button.

■ The Display Properties dialog box appears.

3 Move the mouse ⌖ over the **Settings** tab and then press the left button.

4 To select a new color depth, move the mouse ⌖ over this area and then press the left button.

5 Move the mouse ⌖ over the color depth you want to use and then press the left button.

6 Move the mouse ⌖ over **OK** and then press the left button.

When would I change the number of colors displayed on my screen?

You may want to display more colors on your screen when viewing photographs, playing videos or playing games on your computer.

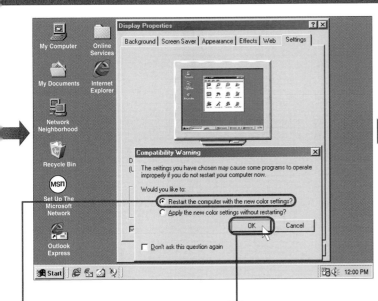

■ A dialog box appears, stating that some programs may not operate properly if you do not restart your computer.

7 To restart your computer with the new color settings, move the mouse ⤢ over this option and then press the left button (○ changes to ⊙).

8 To restart your computer, move the mouse ⤢ over **OK** and then press the left button.

■ A dialog box appears, stating that you must restart your computer before the new settings will take effect.

9 To restart your computer, move the mouse ⤢ over **Yes** and then press the left button.

> You can change the way your mouse works to suit your needs.

CHANGE MOUSE SETTINGS

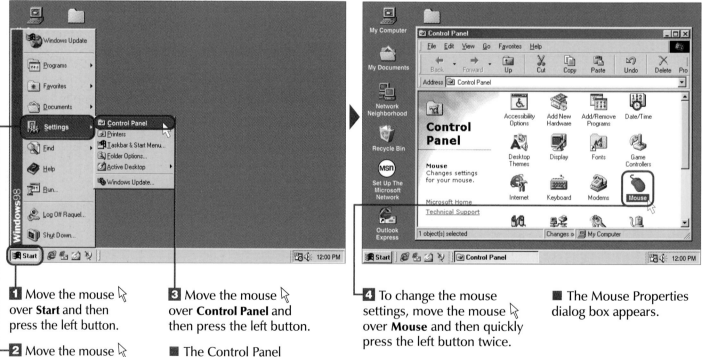

1 Move the mouse over **Start** and then press the left button.

2 Move the mouse over **Settings**.

3 Move the mouse over **Control Panel** and then press the left button.

■ The Control Panel window appears.

4 To change the mouse settings, move the mouse over **Mouse** and then quickly press the left button twice.

■ The Mouse Properties dialog box appears.

Should I use a mouse pad?

A mouse pad provides a smooth surface for moving the mouse on your desk. A mouse pad reduces the amount of dirt that enters the mouse and protects your desk from scratches. Hard plastic mouse pads attract less dirt and provide a smoother surface than fabric mouse pads.

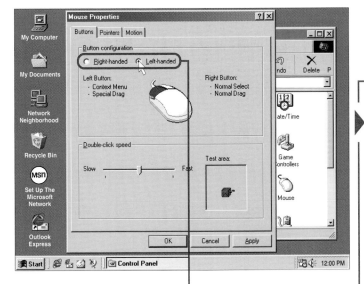

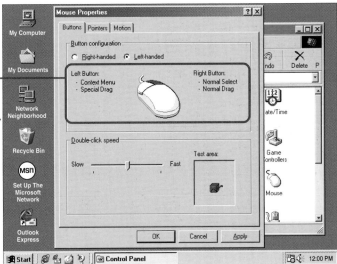

SWITCH BUTTONS

If you are left-handed, you can switch the functions of the left and right mouse buttons to make the mouse easier to use.

1 Move the mouse ░ over an option to specify if you are right-handed or left-handed and then press the left button (○ changes to ⊙).

■ This area describes the functions of the left and right mouse buttons, depending on the option you selected.

CONTINUED➡

You can personalize your mouse by changing the double-click speed and the way the mouse pointer moves on your screen.

CHANGE MOUSE SETTINGS (CONTINUED)

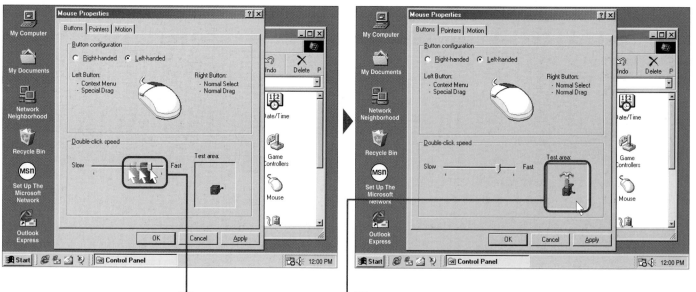

DOUBLE-CLICK SPEED

You can change the amount of time that can pass between two clicks of the mouse button for Windows to recognize a double-click.

1 To change the double-click speed, press and hold down the left button as you drag the slider ( ) to a new position.

2 To test the double-click speed, move the mouse over this area and then quickly press the left button twice.

■ The jack-in-the-box appears if you clicked at the correct speed.

Note: If you are an inexperienced mouse user, you may find a slower speed easier to use.

When should I display pointer trails?

Displaying pointer trails can help you follow the movement of the mouse on your screen. This is especially useful on portable computer screens, where the mouse can be difficult to follow.

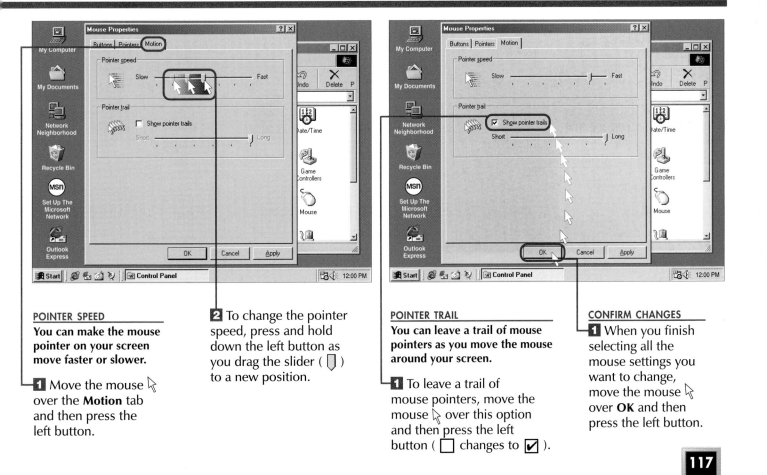

POINTER SPEED

You can make the mouse pointer on your screen move faster or slower.

1 Move the mouse ⌖ over the **Motion** tab and then press the left button.

2 To change the pointer speed, press and hold down the left button as you drag the slider (⬇) to a new position.

POINTER TRAIL

You can leave a trail of mouse pointers as you move the mouse around your screen.

1 To leave a trail of mouse pointers, move the mouse ⌖ over this option and then press the left button (☐ changes to ☑).

CONFIRM CHANGES

1 When you finish selecting all the mouse settings you want to change, move the mouse ⌖ over **OK** and then press the left button.

> You can change the way items on your screen look and act. You can choose the Web style or the Classic style.

CHOOSE THE WEB OR CLASSIC STYLE

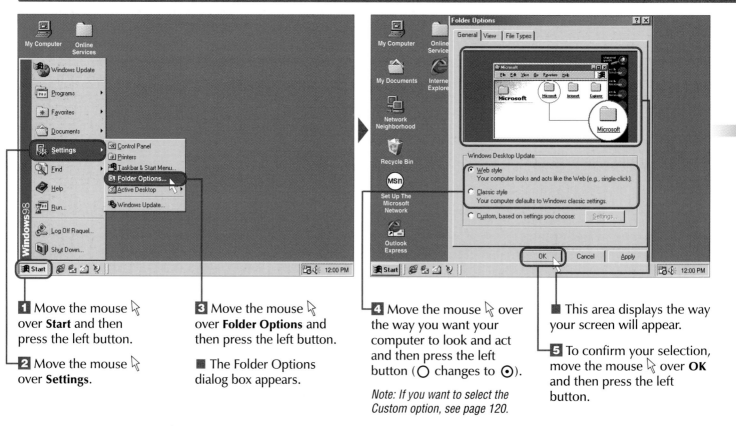

1 Move the mouse ↖ over **Start** and then press the left button.

2 Move the mouse ↖ over **Settings**.

3 Move the mouse ↖ over **Folder Options** and then press the left button.

■ The Folder Options dialog box appears.

4 Move the mouse ↖ over the way you want your computer to look and act and then press the left button (○ changes to ⊙).

Note: If you want to select the Custom option, see page 120.

■ This area displays the way your screen will appear.

5 To confirm your selection, move the mouse ↖ over **OK** and then press the left button.

What is the difference between the Web and Classic style?

Web style

In the Web style, the items on your screen look and act like items on a Web page. You single-click items to open them. You move the mouse over items to select them.

Classic style

In the Classic style, the items on your screen look and act the same way they did in previous versions of Windows. You double-click items to open them. You single-click items to select them.

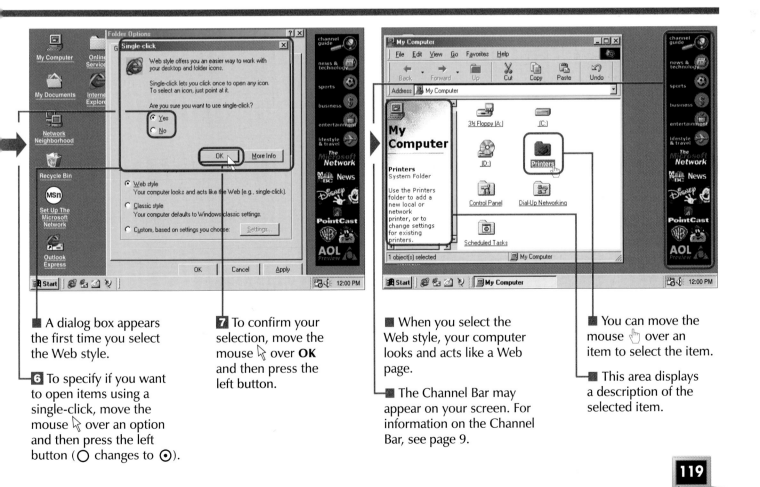

■ A dialog box appears the first time you select the Web style.

6 To specify if you want to open items using a single-click, move the mouse over an option and then press the left button (○ changes to ⊙).

7 To confirm your selection, move the mouse over **OK** and then press the left button.

■ When you select the Web style, your computer looks and acts like a Web page.

■ The Channel Bar may appear on your screen. For information on the Channel Bar, see page 9.

■ You can move the mouse over an item to select the item.

■ This area displays a description of the selected item.

You can mix and match your favorite settings to customize the way items on your screen look and act.

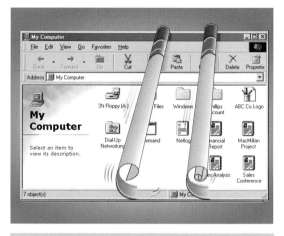

Browse folders

You can choose to open each folder in the same window or in its own window.

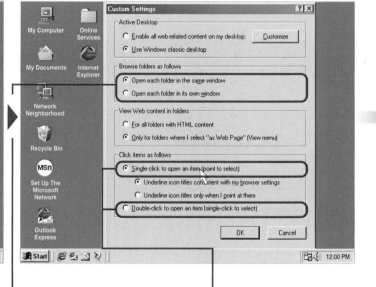

1 To display the Folder Options dialog box, perform steps **1** to **3** on page 118.

2 Move the mouse ⌖ over **Custom** and then press the left button (○ changes to ⊙).

3 To choose your own settings, move the mouse ⌖ over **Settings** and then press the left button.

■ The Custom Settings dialog box appears.

4 To open each folder in the same window or in its own window, move the mouse ⌖ over an option and then press the left button (○ changes to ⊙).

5 To open items using a single-click or a double-click, move the mouse ⌖ over an option and then press the left button (○ changes to ⊙).

Click items

You can choose to open items using a single-click or a double-click.

Single-click
Press the left mouse button once.

Double-click
Quickly press the left mouse button twice.

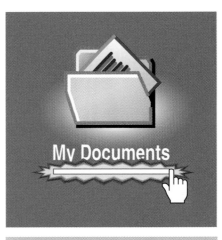

Icon titles

If you choose to open items using a single-click, you can also choose to always underline icon titles or underline icon titles only when you move the mouse over the title.

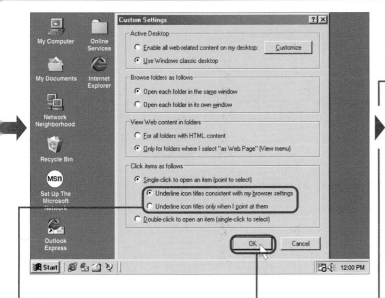

6 If you selected Single-click in step **5**, you can choose to always underline icon titles or underline icon titles only when you position the mouse over the title. Move the mouse over the option you want to use and then press the left button (○ changes to ⊙).

7 To confirm your changes, move the mouse over **OK** and then press the left button.

■ This area displays the way your screen will appear.

8 To close the dialog box, move the mouse over **Close** and then press the left button.

CHAPTER 7

HAVE FUN WITH WINDOWS

Would you like to play games and music CDs on your computer? Do you want to adjust the volume and assign sounds to program events? Find out how in this chapter.

Windows includes several games you can play on your computer. Games are a fun way to improve your mouse skills and hand-eye coordination.

DANGER!!

HIDDEN MINES

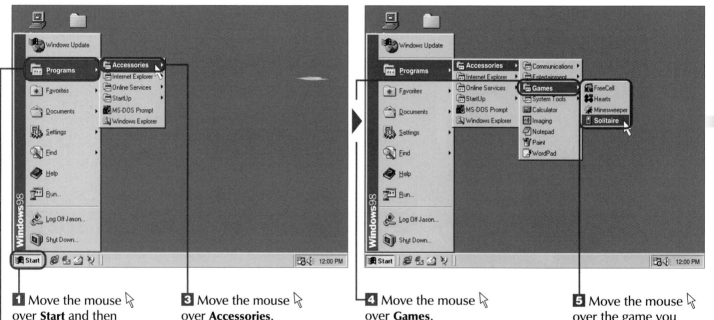

1 Move the mouse over **Start** and then press the left button.

2 Move the mouse over **Programs**.

3 Move the mouse over **Accessories**.

4 Move the mouse over **Games**.

*Note: If **Games** is not available, you must add the Games component to your computer. The Games component is found in the Accessories category. To add a Windows component, see page 158.*

5 Move the mouse over the game you want to play and then press the left button.

124

Does Windows include any other games?

Windows includes two other card games.

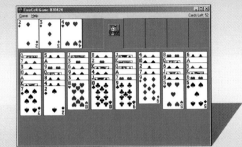

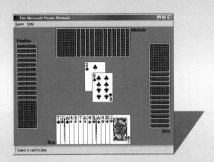

FreeCell

FreeCell is a single-player card game.

Hearts

Hearts is a card game that you can play by yourself or against other people on a network.

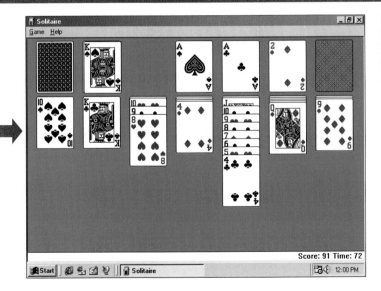

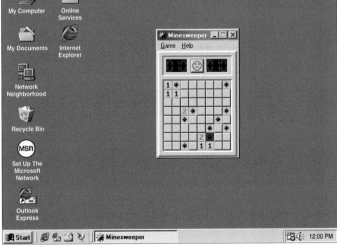

SOLITAIRE

Solitaire is a classic card game that you play on your own. You try to put all the cards in order from ace to king in four stacks, one stack for each suit.

MINESWEEPER

In Minesweeper, you try to locate all of the mines without actually uncovering them.

You can use your computer to play music CDs while you work.

You need a CD-ROM drive, a sound card and speakers to play music CDs.

PLAY A MUSIC CD

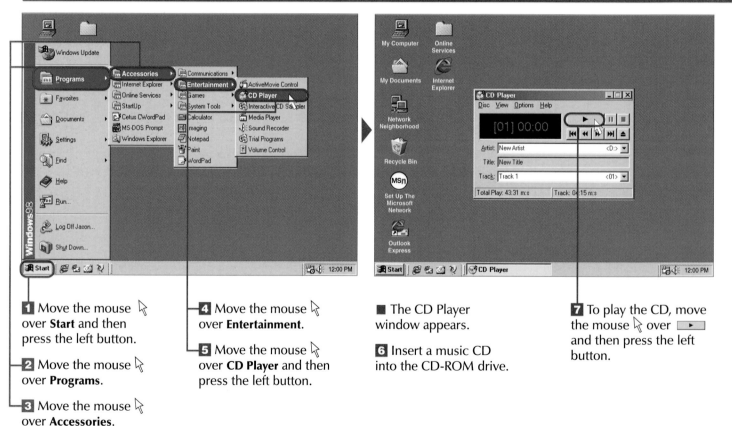

1 Move the mouse over **Start** and then press the left button.

2 Move the mouse over **Programs**.

3 Move the mouse over **Accessories**.

4 Move the mouse over **Entertainment**.

5 Move the mouse over **CD Player** and then press the left button.

■ The CD Player window appears.

6 Insert a music CD into the CD-ROM drive.

7 To play the CD, move the mouse over ▶ and then press the left button.

Can I listen to music privately?

You can listen to music privately by plugging a headset into your CD-ROM drive.

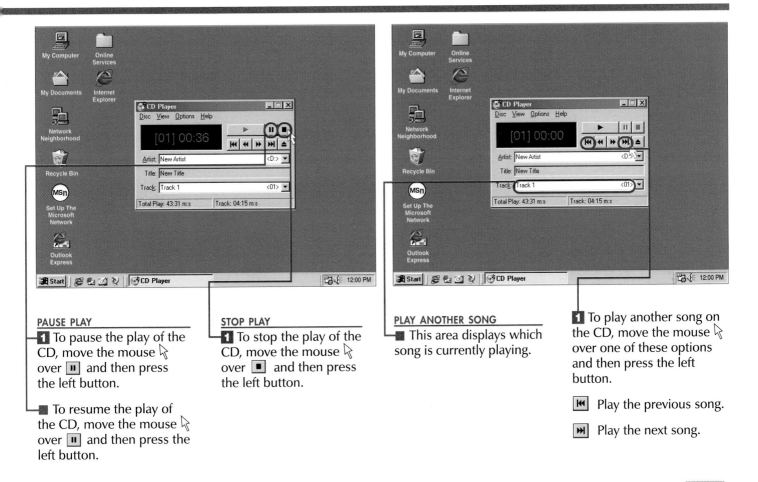

PAUSE PLAY

1 To pause the play of the CD, move the mouse over [II] and then press the left button.

To resume the play of the CD, move the mouse over [II] and then press the left button.

STOP PLAY

1 To stop the play of the CD, move the mouse over [■] and then press the left button.

PLAY ANOTHER SONG

This area displays which song is currently playing.

1 To play another song on the CD, move the mouse over one of these options and then press the left button.

[◄◄] Play the previous song.

[►►] Play the next song.

You can have Windows play the songs on a CD in random order.

PLAY A MUSIC CD (CONTINUED)

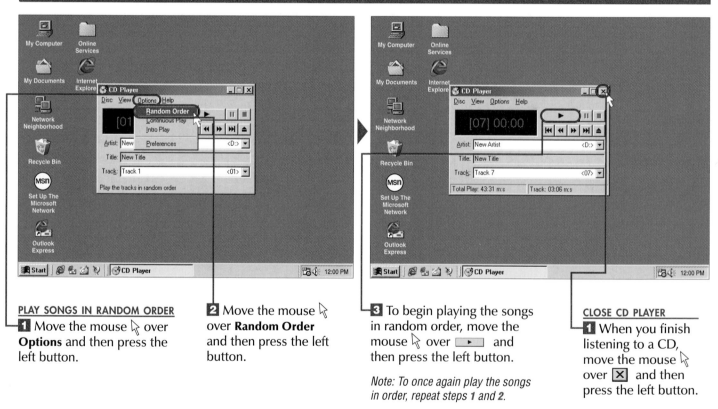

PLAY SONGS IN RANDOM ORDER

1 Move the mouse ❳ over **Options** and then press the left button.

2 Move the mouse ❳ over **Random Order** and then press the left button.

3 To begin playing the songs in random order, move the mouse ❳ over ▶ and then press the left button.

Note: To once again play the songs in order, repeat steps 1 and 2.

CLOSE CD PLAYER

1 When you finish listening to a CD, move the mouse ❳ over ☒ and then press the left button.

You can easily adjust the volume of sound coming from your speakers.

ADJUST THE VOLUME

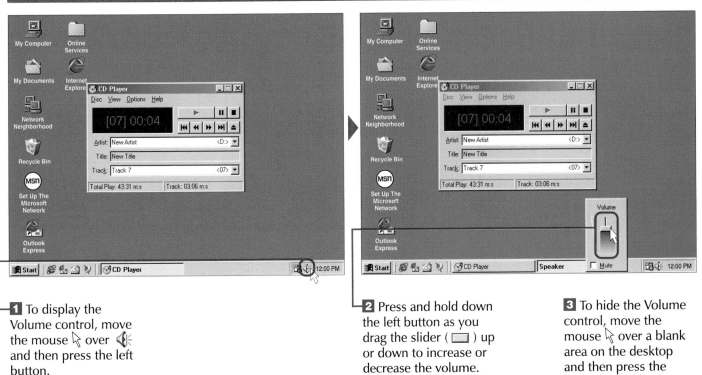

1 To display the Volume control, move the mouse ⩗ over ⵏⵏ and then press the left button.

2 Press and hold down the left button as you drag the slider (▭) up or down to increase or decrease the volume.

3 To hide the Volume control, move the mouse ⩗ over a blank area on the desktop and then press the left button.

You can have Windows play sound effects when you perform certain tasks on your computer.

For example, you can hear a tambourine when you empty the Recycle Bin or thunder when you exit Windows.

ASSIGN A SOUND SCHEME

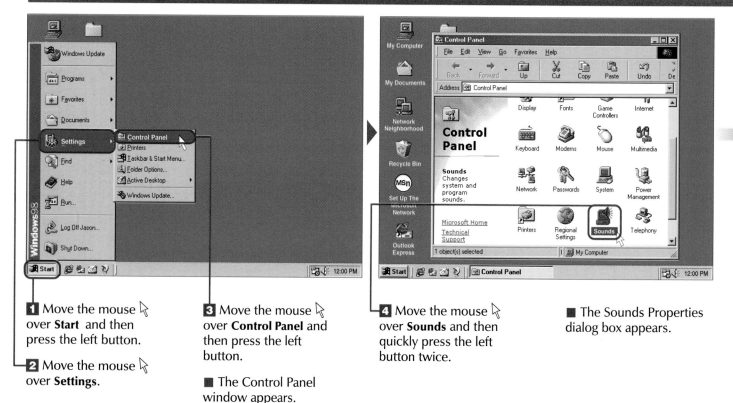

1 Move the mouse over **Start** and then press the left button.

2 Move the mouse over **Settings**.

3 Move the mouse over **Control Panel** and then press the left button.

■ The Control Panel window appears.

4 Move the mouse over **Sounds** and then quickly press the left button twice.

■ The Sounds Properties dialog box appears.

How can I get more sound schemes?

Windows includes other sound schemes you can install by adding the Multimedia Sound Schemes component, found in the Multimedia category. To add a Windows component, see page 158.

Windows includes these sound schemes:

Jungle   Musica   Robotz   Utopia

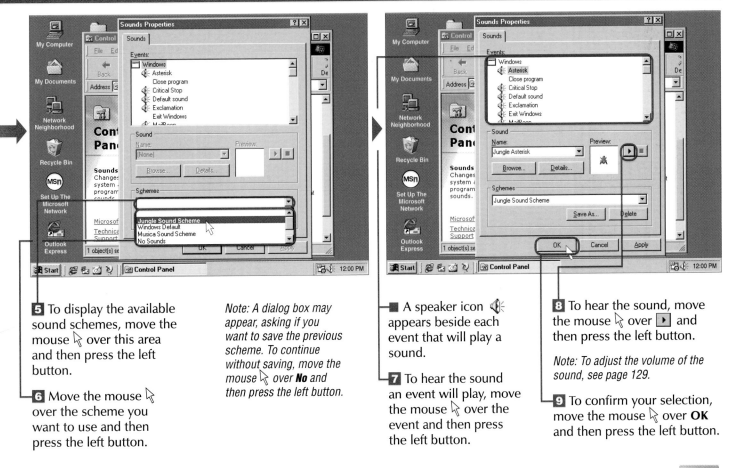

5 To display the available sound schemes, move the mouse over this area and then press the left button.

6 Move the mouse over the scheme you want to use and then press the left button.

*Note: A dialog box may appear, asking if you want to save the previous scheme. To continue without saving, move the mouse over **No** and then press the left button.*

■ A speaker icon appears beside each event that will play a sound.

7 To hear the sound an event will play, move the mouse over the event and then press the left button.

8 To hear the sound, move the mouse over ▶ and then press the left button.

Note: To adjust the volume of the sound, see page 129.

9 To confirm your selection, move the mouse over **OK** and then press the left button.

You can assign a sound to an event performed on your computer.

You may want to hear your favorite cartoon character each time you close a program or a sigh of relief when you restore a window. You need a sound card and speakers to hear sounds on your computer.

ASSIGN A SOUND TO ONE EVENT

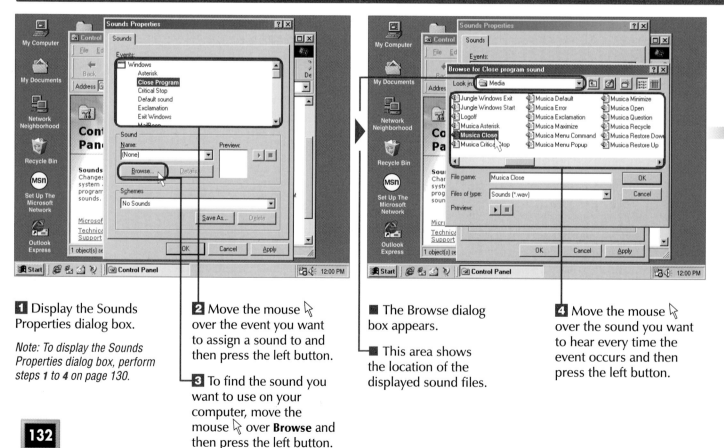

1 Display the Sounds Properties dialog box.

Note: To display the Sounds Properties dialog box, perform steps 1 to 4 on page 130.

2 Move the mouse over the event you want to assign a sound to and then press the left button.

3 To find the sound you want to use on your computer, move the mouse over **Browse** and then press the left button.

■ The Browse dialog box appears.

■ This area shows the location of the displayed sound files.

4 Move the mouse over the sound you want to hear every time the event occurs and then press the left button.

Where can I get sounds?

You can purchase sounds at computer stores or get sounds on the Internet. Make sure you use sounds with the .wav extension, such as wolfhowl.wav.

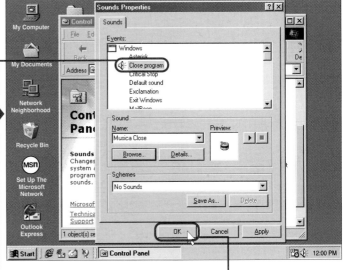

5 To play the sound you selected, move the mouse ↳ over ▶ and then press the left button.

6 To select the sound, move the mouse ↳ over **OK** and then press the left button.

■ A speaker icon (📢) appears beside the event.

7 To assign sounds to other events, repeat steps **2** to **6** for each event.

8 To confirm your changes, move the mouse ↳ over **OK** and then press the left button.

CHAPTER 8

OPTIMIZE YOUR COMPUTER

What can I do to improve the performance of my computer? Read this chapter and learn how to complete tasks such as deleting unnecessary files and repairing disk errors.

You must format a floppy disk before you can use the disk to store information.

Floppy disks you buy at computer stores are usually formatted. You may want to later format a disk again to erase the information it contains and prepare the disk for storing new information.

FORMAT A FLOPPY DISK

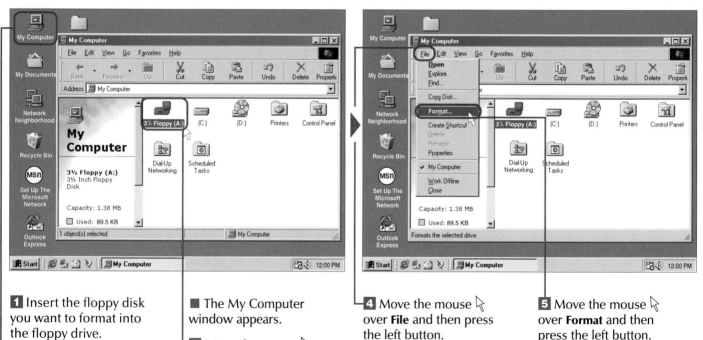

1 Insert the floppy disk you want to format into the floppy drive.

2 Move the mouse over **My Computer** and then quickly press the left button twice.

■ The My Computer window appears.

3 Move the mouse over the drive containing the floppy disk you want to format (example: **A:**) and then press the left button.

4 Move the mouse over **File** and then press the left button.

5 Move the mouse over **Format** and then press the left button.

■ The Format dialog box appears.

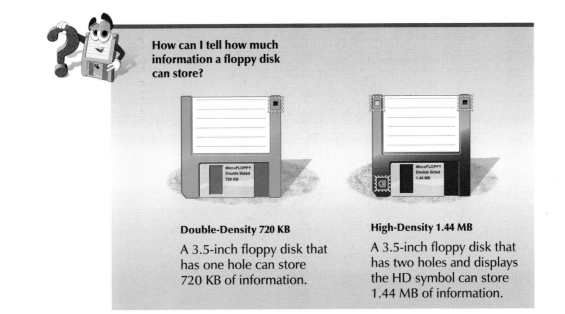

How can I tell how much information a floppy disk can store?

Double-Density 720 KB

A 3.5-inch floppy disk that has one hole can store 720 KB of information.

High-Density 1.44 MB

A 3.5-inch floppy disk that has two holes and displays the HD symbol can store 1.44 MB of information.

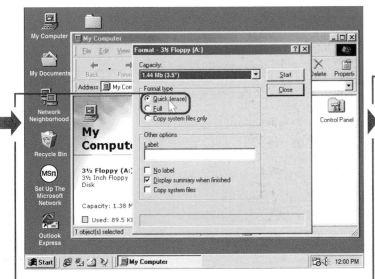

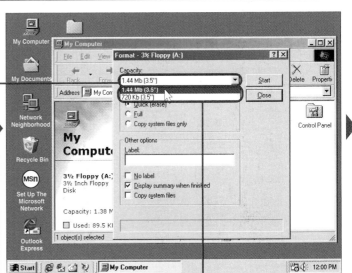

6 Move the mouse ▷ over the type of format you want to perform and then press the left button (○ changes to ⊙).

*Note: If the floppy disk has never been formatted, select the **Full** option.*

Quick (erase)
Removes all files but does not scan the disk for damaged areas.

Full
Removes all files and scans the disk for damaged areas.

7 To specify how much information the floppy disk can store, move the mouse ▷ over this area and then press the left button.

8 Move the mouse ▷ over the storage capacity of the floppy disk and then press the left button.

CONTINUED

Before formatting a floppy disk, make sure the disk does not contain information you may need. Formatting a floppy disk will permanently remove all the information on the disk.

FORMAT A FLOPPY DISK (CONTINUED)

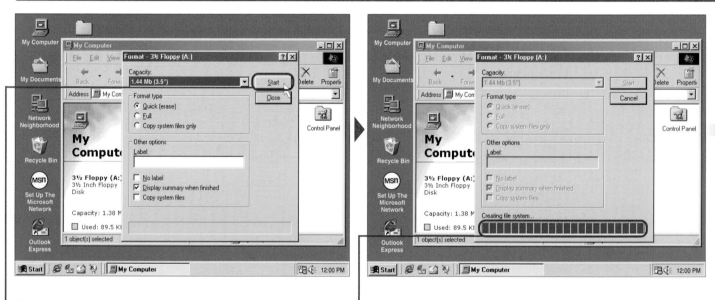

9 To start formatting the floppy disk, move the mouse ⬚ over **Start** and then press the left button.

■ This area displays the progress of the format.

How can I tell if a floppy disk is formatted?

Windows will tell you if a floppy disk is not formatted when you try to view the contents of the disk. You cannot tell if a floppy disk is formatted just by looking at the disk.

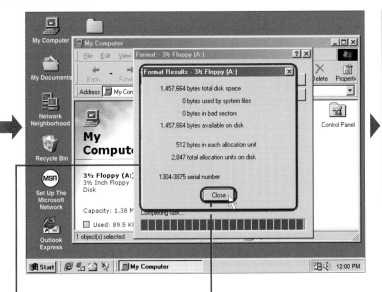

■ The Format Results dialog box appears when the format is complete. The dialog box displays information about the formatted disk.

10 When you finish viewing the information, move the mouse ⊳ over **Close** and then press the left button.

■ To format another floppy disk, insert the disk and then repeat steps **6** to **10** starting on page 137.

11 To close the Format dialog box, move the mouse ⊳ over **Close** and then press the left button.

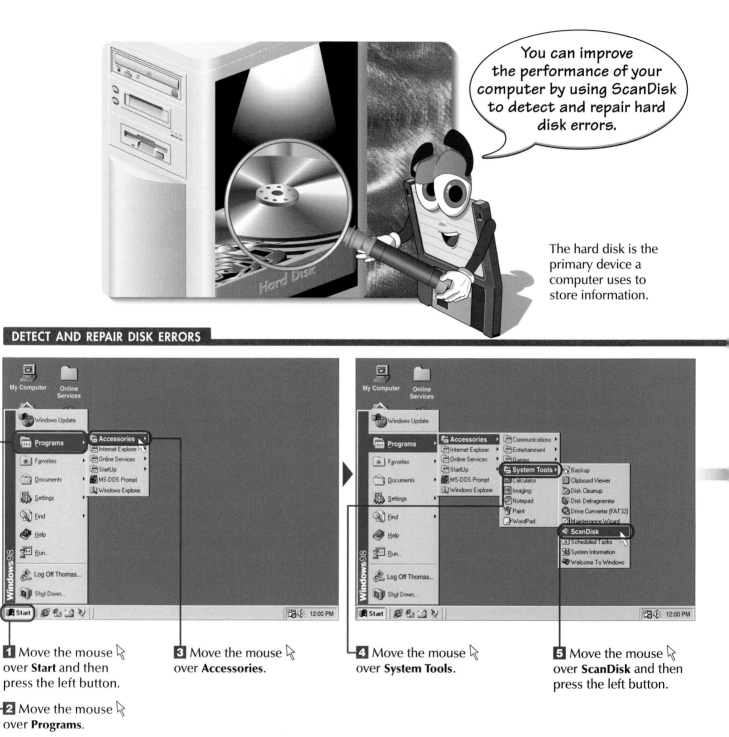

You can improve the performance of your computer by using ScanDisk to detect and repair hard disk errors.

The hard disk is the primary device a computer uses to store information.

DETECT AND REPAIR DISK ERRORS

1 Move the mouse over **Start** and then press the left button.

2 Move the mouse over **Programs**.

3 Move the mouse over **Accessories**.

4 Move the mouse over **System Tools**.

5 Move the mouse over **ScanDisk** and then press the left button.

How often should I check my hard disk for errors?

You should check your hard disk for errors at least once a month. You can set up Windows to check for hard disk errors and perform other tasks on a regular basis. See page 154.

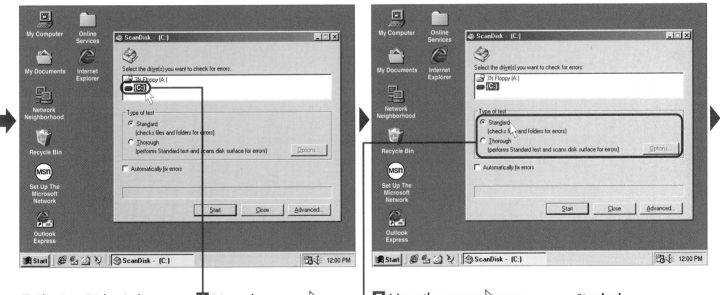

■ The ScanDisk window appears.

6 Move the mouse ⌖ over the disk you want to check for errors (example: **C:**) and then press the left button.

7 Move the mouse ⌖ over the type of test you want to perform and then press the left button (○ changes to ⊙).

Standard
Checks files and folders for errors.

Thorough
Checks files, folders and the disk surface for errors.

CONT☺NUED➡

DETECT AND REPAIR DISK ERRORS (CONTINUED)

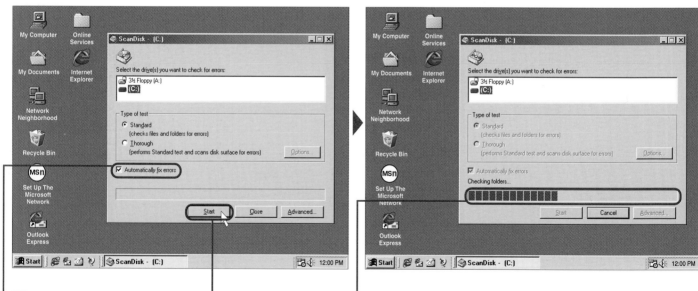

8 If you want Windows to automatically repair any disk errors it finds, move the mouse ⬚ over this option and then press the left button (☐ changes to ☑).

9 To start the check, move the mouse ⬚ over **Start** and then press the left button.

■ This area displays the progress of the check.

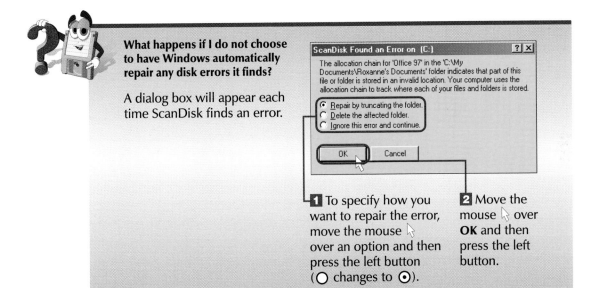

What happens if I do not choose to have Windows automatically repair any disk errors it finds?

A dialog box will appear each time ScanDisk finds an error.

ScanDisk Found an Error on [C:]

The allocation chain for 'Office 97' in the 'C:\My Documents\Roxanne's Documents' folder indicates that part of this file or folder is stored in an invalid location. Your computer uses the allocation chain to track where each of your files and folders is stored.

◉ Repair by truncating the folder.
○ Delete the affected folder.
○ Ignore this error and continue.

OK   Cancel

1 To specify how you want to repair the error, move the mouse over an option and then press the left button (○ changes to ◉).

2 Move the mouse over **OK** and then press the left button.

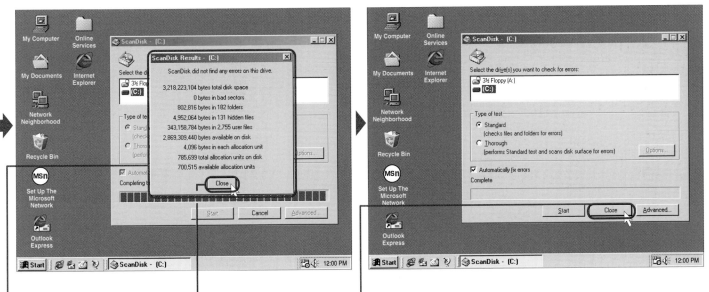

■ The ScanDisk Results dialog box appears when the check is complete. The dialog box displays information about the disk.

10 When you finish viewing the information, move the mouse over **Close** and then press the left button.

11 To close the ScanDisk window, move the mouse over **Close** and then press the left button.

You can improve the performance of your computer by defragmenting your hard disk.

A fragmented hard disk stores parts of a file in many different locations. Your computer must search many areas on the disk to retrieve a file.

DEFRAGMENT YOUR HARD DISK

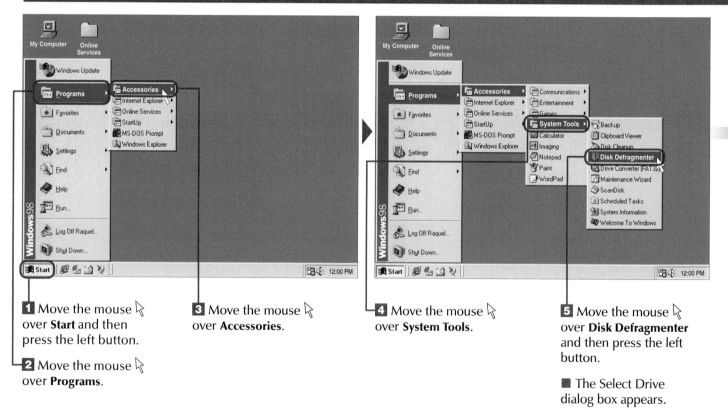

1 Move the mouse ⬚ over **Start** and then press the left button.

2 Move the mouse ⬚ over **Programs**.

3 Move the mouse ⬚ over **Accessories**.

4 Move the mouse ⬚ over **System Tools**.

5 Move the mouse ⬚ over **Disk Defragmenter** and then press the left button.

■ The Select Drive dialog box appears.

You can use Disk Defragmenter to place all the parts of a file in one location. This reduces the time your computer will spend locating the file.

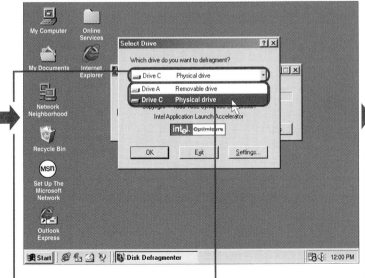

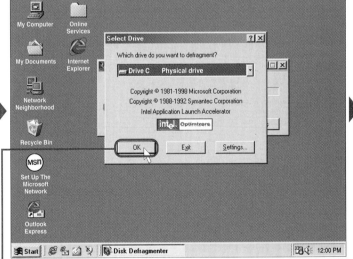

6 To display a list of the drives you can defragment, move the mouse ⬚ over this area and then press the left button.

7 Move the mouse ⬚ over the drive you want to defragment and then press the left button.

8 To start the defragmentation, move the mouse ⬚ over **OK** and then press the left button.

CONT©NUED➡

You can perform other tasks on your computer while Windows defragments your hard disk, but your computer will operate slower and the defragmentation will take longer.

The defragmentation process must restart each time a program stores information on your hard disk. You may want to close all other programs to speed up the defragmentation.

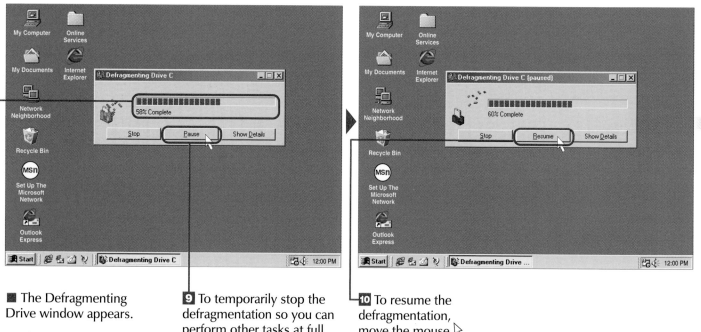

■ The Defragmenting Drive window appears.

■ This area displays the progress of the defragmentation.

9 To temporarily stop the defragmentation so you can perform other tasks at full speed, move the mouse over **Pause** and then press the left button.

10 To resume the defragmentation, move the mouse over **Resume** and then press the left button.

How often should I defragment my hard disk?

You should defragment your hard disk at least once a month. You can set up Windows to defragment your hard disk and perform other computer maintenance tasks on a regular basis. See page 154.

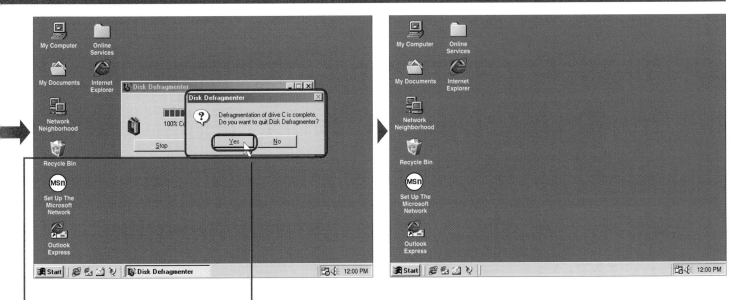

■ A dialog box appears when the defragmentation is complete.

11 To close Disk Defragmenter, move the mouse ↖ over **Yes** and then press the left button.

■ You can now use your computer as usual.

Disk Cleanup will remove unnecessary files from your computer to free up disk space.

USING DISK CLEANUP

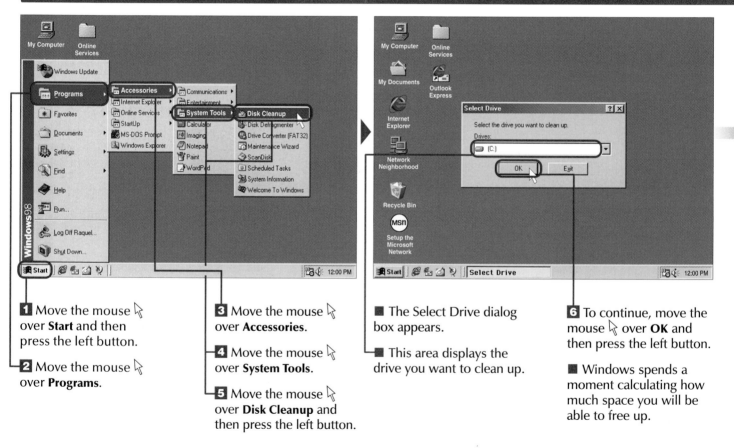

1 Move the mouse over **Start** and then press the left button.

2 Move the mouse over **Programs**.

3 Move the mouse over **Accessories**.

4 Move the mouse over **System Tools**.

5 Move the mouse over **Disk Cleanup** and then press the left button.

■ The Select Drive dialog box appears.

■ This area displays the drive you want to clean up.

6 To continue, move the mouse over **OK** and then press the left button.

■ Windows spends a moment calculating how much space you will be able to free up.

**What types of files can
Disk Cleanup remove?**

Temporary Internet Files
Web pages stored on
your computer for
quick viewing.

Downloaded Program File
Information transferred
from the Internet when
you view certain Web
pages.

Recycle Bin
Files you have
deleted.

Temporary Files
Files created by
programs for
storing temporary
information.

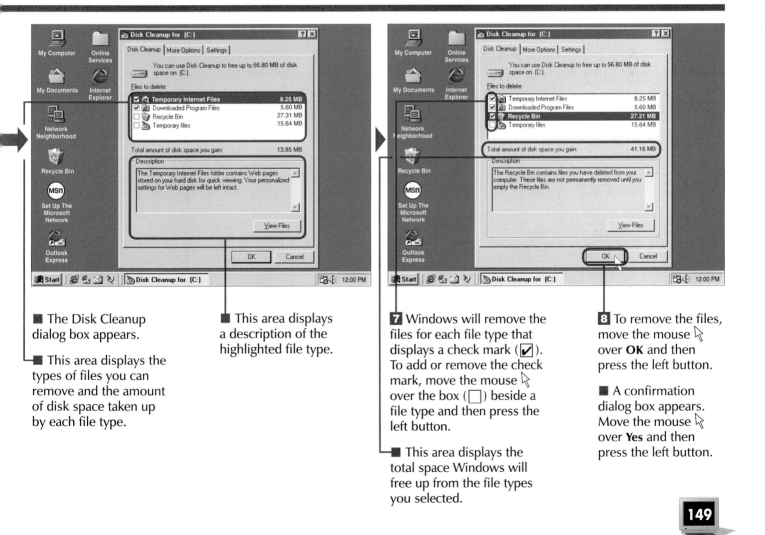

■ The Disk Cleanup
dialog box appears.

■ This area displays the
types of files you can
remove and the amount
of disk space taken up
by each file type.

■ This area displays
a description of the
highlighted file type.

7 Windows will remove the
files for each file type that
displays a check mark (✔).
To add or remove the check
mark, move the mouse ⬚
over the box (☐) beside a
file type and then press the
left button.

■ This area displays the
total space Windows will
free up from the file types
you selected.

8 To remove the files,
move the mouse ⬚
over **OK** and then
press the left button.

■ A confirmation
dialog box appears.
Move the mouse ⬚
over **Yes** and then
press the left button.

You can use Task Scheduler to have Windows automatically perform tasks on a regular basis. This is useful for running computer maintenance programs such as Disk Defragmenter or ScanDisk.

SCHEDULE TASKS

1 Move the mouse ⌖ over **Start** and then press the left button.

2 Move the mouse ⌖ over **Programs**.

3 Move the mouse ⌖ over **Accessories**.

4 Move the mouse ⌖ over **System Tools**.

5 Move the mouse ⌖ over **Scheduled Tasks** and then press the left button.

■ The Scheduled Tasks window appears.

6 To schedule a new program, move the mouse ⌖ over **Add Scheduled Task** and then quickly press the left button twice.

How does Task Scheduler know when to start a program?

Task Scheduler uses the date and time set in your computer to determine when to start a scheduled task. Before you schedule a task, make sure this information is correct. See page 100 to change the date and time set in your computer.

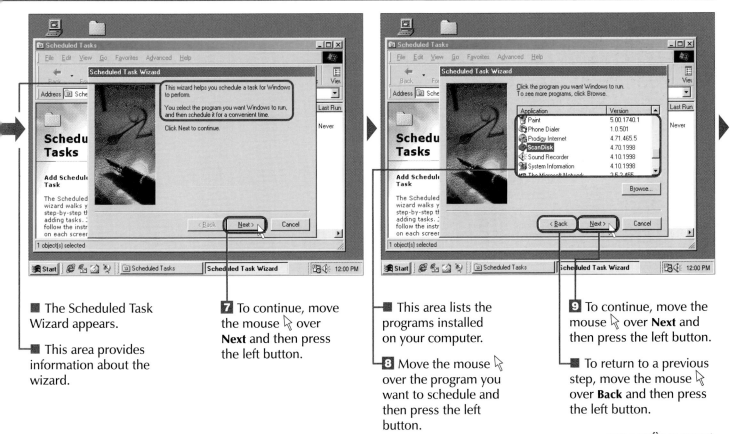

■ The Scheduled Task Wizard appears.

■ This area provides information about the wizard.

7 To continue, move the mouse Ⓚ over **Next** and then press the left button.

■ This area lists the programs installed on your computer.

8 Move the mouse Ⓚ over the program you want to schedule and then press the left button.

9 To continue, move the mouse Ⓚ over **Next** and then press the left button.

■ To return to a previous step, move the mouse Ⓚ over **Back** and then press the left button.

CONTINUED➡

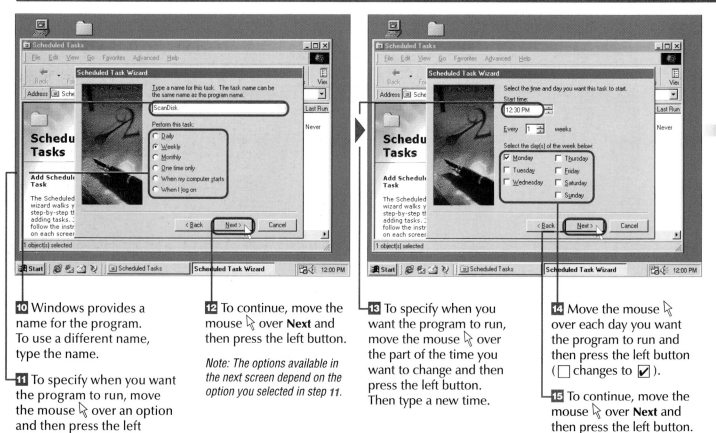

10 Windows provides a name for the program. To use a different name, type the name.

11 To specify when you want the program to run, move the mouse ⬚ over an option and then press the left button (○ changes to ◉).

12 To continue, move the mouse ⬚ over **Next** and then press the left button.

Note: The options available in the next screen depend on the option you selected in step 11.

13 To specify when you want the program to run, move the mouse ⬚ over the part of the time you want to change and then press the left button. Then type a new time.

14 Move the mouse ⬚ over each day you want the program to run and then press the left button (☐ changes to ☑).

15 To continue, move the mouse ⬚ over **Next** and then press the left button.

Can I remove a task so it will no longer run automatically?

Yes. In the Scheduled Tasks window, move the mouse ⬆ over the program you want to remove and then press the left button. Press the `Delete` key to remove the task. To confirm the deletion, move the mouse ⬆ over **Yes** and then press the left button. Deleting a program from Task Scheduler does not remove the program from your computer.

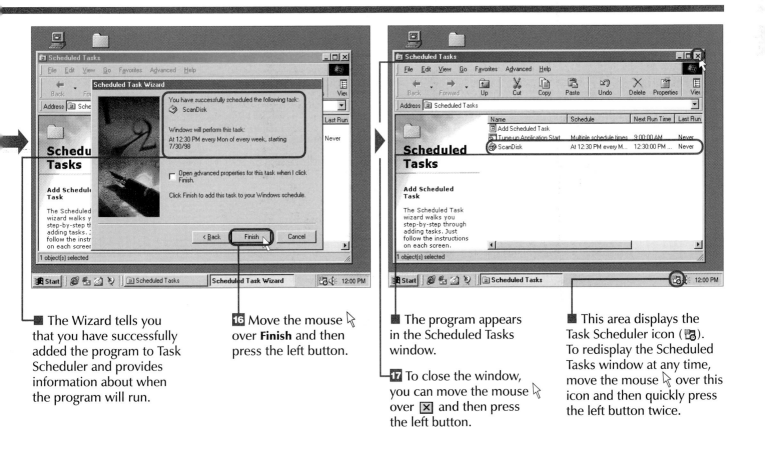

◼ The Wizard tells you that you have successfully added the program to Task Scheduler and provides information about when the program will run.

16 Move the mouse ⬆ over **Finish** and then press the left button.

◼ The program appears in the Scheduled Tasks window.

17 To close the window, you can move the mouse ⬆ over ✕ and then press the left button.

◼ This area displays the Task Scheduler icon (🖳). To redisplay the Scheduled Tasks window at any time, move the mouse ⬆ over this icon and then quickly press the left button twice.

You can schedule regular maintenance tasks to optimize the performance of your computer.

USING THE MAINTENANCE WIZARD

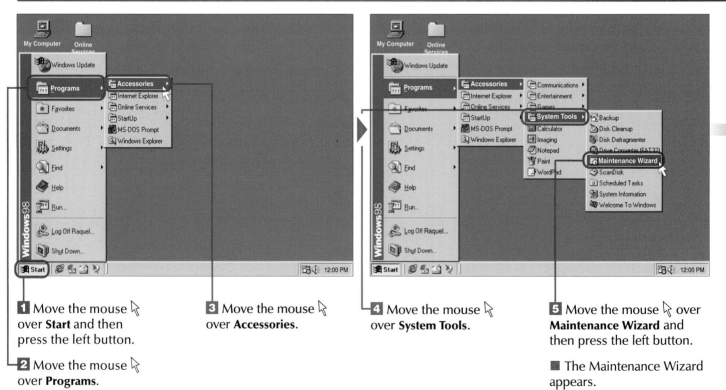

1 Move the mouse over **Start** and then press the left button.

2 Move the mouse over **Programs**.

3 Move the mouse over **Accessories**.

4 Move the mouse over **System Tools**.

5 Move the mouse over **Maintenance Wizard** and then press the left button.

■ The Maintenance Wizard appears.

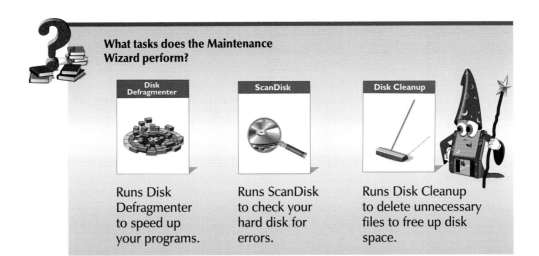

What tasks does the Maintenance Wizard perform?

Disk Defragmenter

Runs Disk Defragmenter to speed up your programs.

ScanDisk

Runs ScanDisk to check your hard disk for errors.

Disk Cleanup

Runs Disk Cleanup to delete unnecessary files to free up disk space.

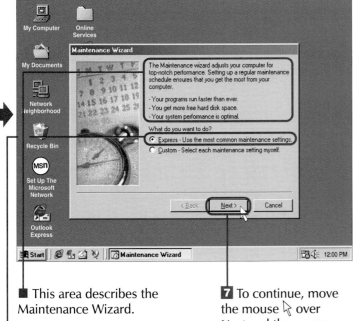

■ This area describes the Maintenance Wizard.

◼6◼ To use the most common maintenance settings, move the mouse ▷ over **Express** and then press the left button (○ changes to ⊙).

◼7◼ To continue, move the mouse ▷ over **Next** and then press the left button.

◼8◼ To select when you want to schedule your maintenance tasks, move the mouse ▷ over an option and then press the left button (○ changes to ⊙).

◼9◼ To continue, move the mouse ▷ over **Next** and then press the left button.

CONTINUED➡

Your computer must be on when the scheduled maintenance tasks will run.

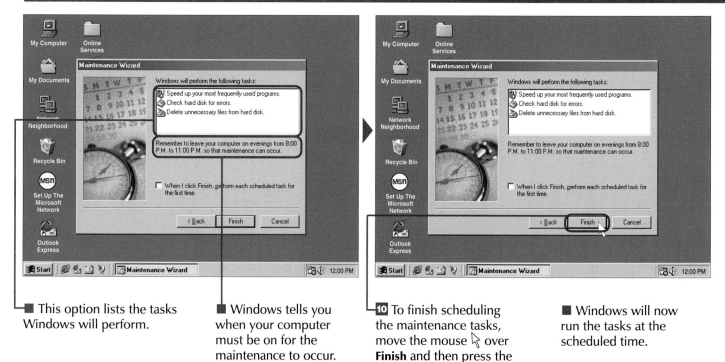

■ This option lists the tasks Windows will perform.

■ Windows tells you when your computer must be on for the maintenance to occur.

🔟 To finish scheduling the maintenance tasks, move the mouse ⍾ over **Finish** and then press the left button.

■ Windows will now run the tasks at the scheduled time.

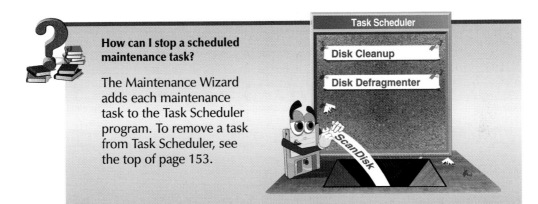

How can I stop a scheduled maintenance task?

The Maintenance Wizard adds each maintenance task to the Task Scheduler program. To remove a task from Task Scheduler, see the top of page 153.

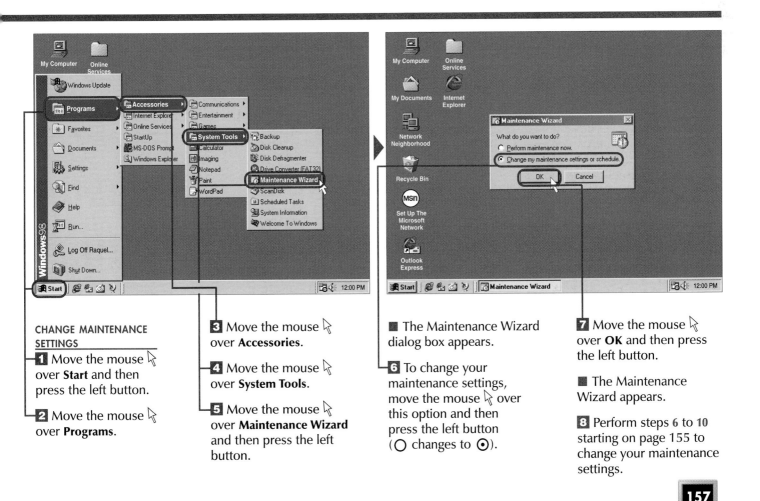

CHANGE MAINTENANCE SETTINGS

1 Move the mouse ⌖ over **Start** and then press the left button.

2 Move the mouse ⌖ over **Programs**.

3 Move the mouse ⌖ over **Accessories**.

4 Move the mouse ⌖ over **System Tools**.

5 Move the mouse ⌖ over **Maintenance Wizard** and then press the left button.

■ The Maintenance Wizard dialog box appears.

6 To change your maintenance settings, move the mouse ⌖ over this option and then press the left button (○ changes to ⊙).

7 Move the mouse ⌖ over **OK** and then press the left button.

■ The Maintenance Wizard appears.

8 Perform steps **6** to **10** starting on page 155 to change your maintenance settings.

157

You can add components to your computer that were not added when you first set up Windows.

When setting up Windows, most people do not install all the components that come with the program. This prevents unneeded components from taking up storage space on the computer.

ADD WINDOWS COMPONENTS

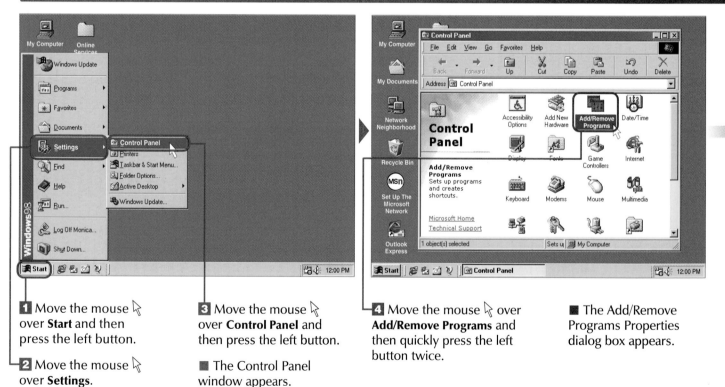

1 Move the mouse over **Start** and then press the left button.

2 Move the mouse over **Settings**.

3 Move the mouse over **Control Panel** and then press the left button.

■ The Control Panel window appears.

4 Move the mouse over **Add/Remove Programs** and then quickly press the left button twice.

■ The Add/Remove Programs Properties dialog box appears.

Which Windows components can I add to my computer?

Windows components you can add to your computer include:

Games

Provides entertaining games such as Minesweeper and Solitaire.

Desktop Themes

Allows you to customize your desktop with a particular theme, such as a baseball or jungle theme.

Multimedia Sound Schemes

Provides sound effects Windows can play when you perform certain tasks on your computer.

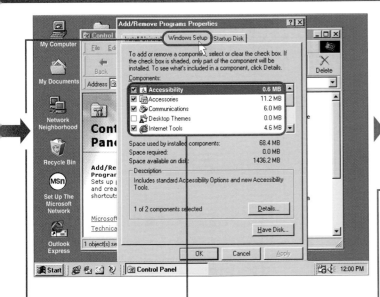

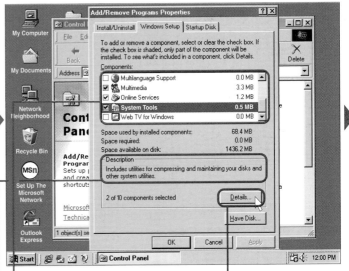

5 Move the mouse over the **Windows Setup** tab and then press the left button.

Note: Windows may take a moment to display the information.

■ This area displays the categories of components you can add to your computer.

■ The box beside each category indicates if all (☑), some (☑) or none (☐) of the components in the category are installed on your computer.

6 To display a description of the components in a category, move the mouse over the category and then press the left button.

■ This area displays a description of the components in the category.

7 To display the components in the category, move the mouse over **Details** and then press the left button.

CONTINUED

When adding Windows components, you will be asked to insert the CD-ROM disc you used to install Windows.
Microsoft Windows98
NEW VERSION!

ADD WINDOWS COMPONENTS (CONTINUED)

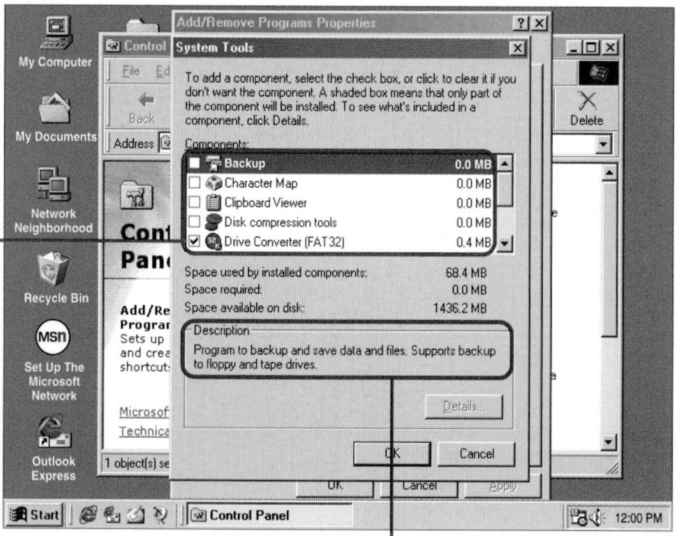
Add/Remove Programs Properties
System Tools
To add a component, select the check box, or click to clear it if you don't want the component. A shaded box means that only part of the component will be installed. To see what's included in a component, click Details.
Components:
Backup 0.0 MB
Character Map 0.0 MB
Clipboard Viewer 0.0 MB
Disk compression tools 0.0 MB
Drive Converter (FAT32) 0.4 MB
Space used by installed components: 68.4 MB
Space required: 0.0 MB
Space available on disk: 1436.2 MB
Description
Program to backup and save data and files. Supports backup to floppy and tape drives.
Details...
OK
Cancel
Start
Control Panel
12:00 PM

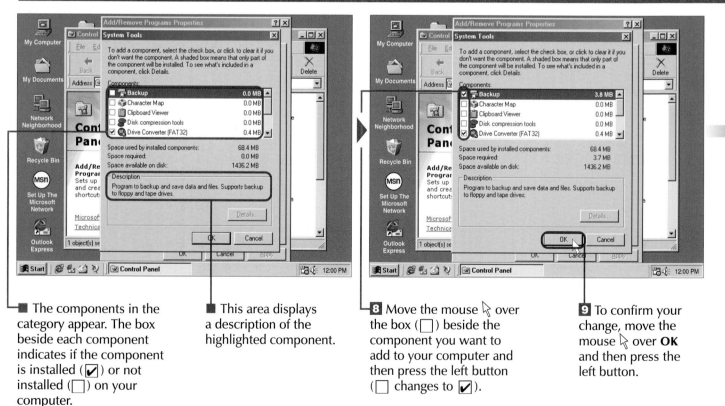

■ The components in the category appear. The box beside each component indicates if the component is installed (☑) or not installed (☐) on your computer.

■ This area displays a description of the highlighted component.

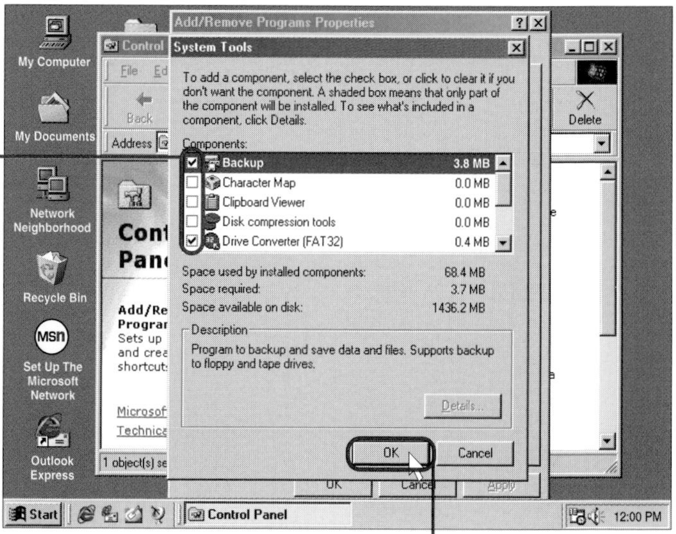
Add/Remove Programs Properties
System Tools
To add a component, select the check box, or click to clear it if you don't want the component. A shaded box means that only part of the component will be installed. To see what's included in a component, click Details.
Components:
Backup 3.8 MB
Character Map 0.0 MB
Clipboard Viewer 0.0 MB
Disk compression tools 0.0 MB
Drive Converter (FAT32) 0.4 MB
Space used by installed components: 68.4 MB
Space required: 3.7 MB
Space available on disk: 1436.2 MB
Description
Program to backup and save data and files. Supports backup to floppy and tape drives.
Details...
OK
Cancel
Start
Control Panel
12:00 PM

8 Move the mouse over the box (☐) beside the component you want to add to your computer and then press the left button (☐ changes to ☑).

9 To confirm your change, move the mouse over **OK** and then press the left button.

How do I remove a component I do not use?

You can remove a component you do not use by performing steps 1 to 10 starting on page 158. When you select a component you want to remove, ☑ changes to ☐ in step 8.

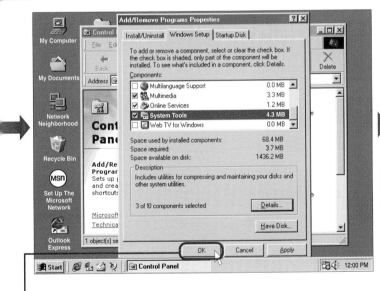

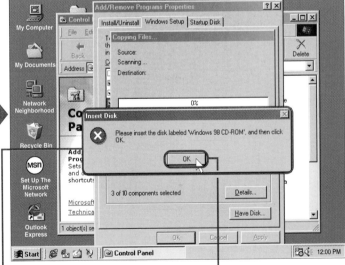

10 To close the Add/Remove Programs Properties dialog box, move the mouse ↖ over **OK** and then press the left button.

■ The Insert Disk dialog box appears, asking you to insert the Windows 98 CD-ROM disc.

11 Insert the CD-ROM disc into the drive.

12 To continue, move the mouse ↖ over **OK** and then press the left button.

Note: Windows may ask you to restart your computer.

161

Before you can use a new printer, you need to install the printer on your computer. Windows includes a wizard that guides you step-by-step through the process of installing a new printer.

You will need the Windows 98 CD-ROM disc to install a new printer.

INSTALL A PRINTER

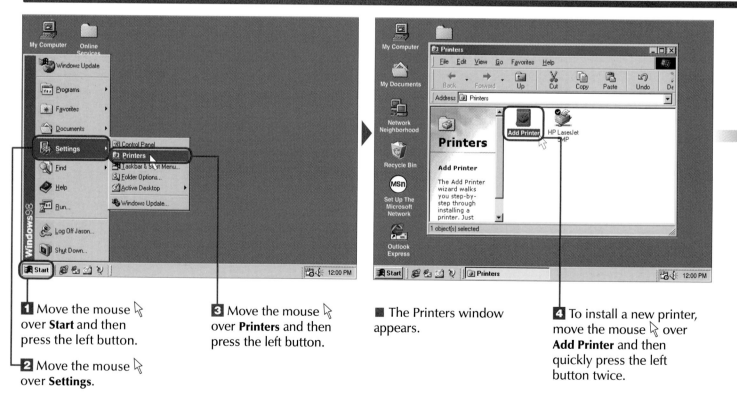

1 Move the mouse ⌖ over **Start** and then press the left button.

2 Move the mouse ⌖ over **Settings**.

3 Move the mouse ⌖ over **Printers** and then press the left button.

■ The Printers window appears.

4 To install a new printer, move the mouse ⌖ over **Add Printer** and then quickly press the left button twice.

What is the difference between a local printer and a network printer?

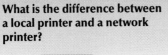

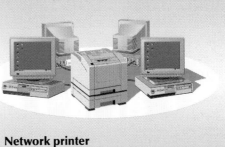

Local printer

Printer connects directly to your computer.

Network printer

Printer connects to multiple computers on the network.

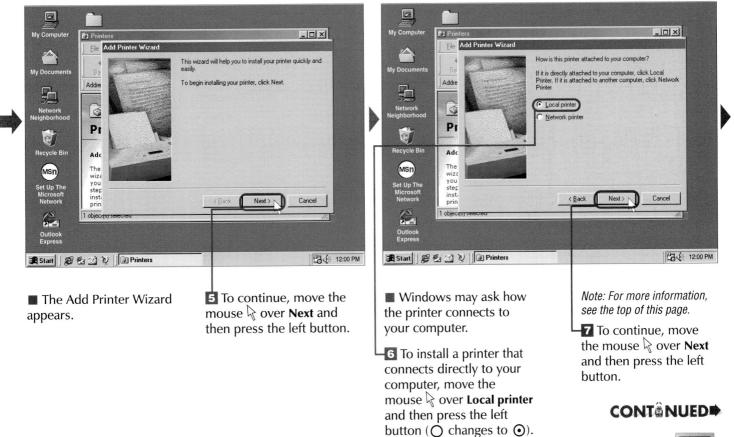

■ The Add Printer Wizard appears.

5 To continue, move the mouse ⬚ over **Next** and then press the left button.

■ Windows may ask how the printer connects to your computer.

6 To install a printer that connects directly to your computer, move the mouse ⬚ over **Local printer** and then press the left button (○ changes to ⊙).

Note: For more information, see the top of this page.

7 To continue, move the mouse ⬚ over **Next** and then press the left button.

CONTINUED

When installing a printer, you must specify the manufacturer and model of the printer.

Manufacturer:
Hewlett-Packard

Model:
HP LaserJet 5M

INSTALL A PRINTER (CONTINUED)

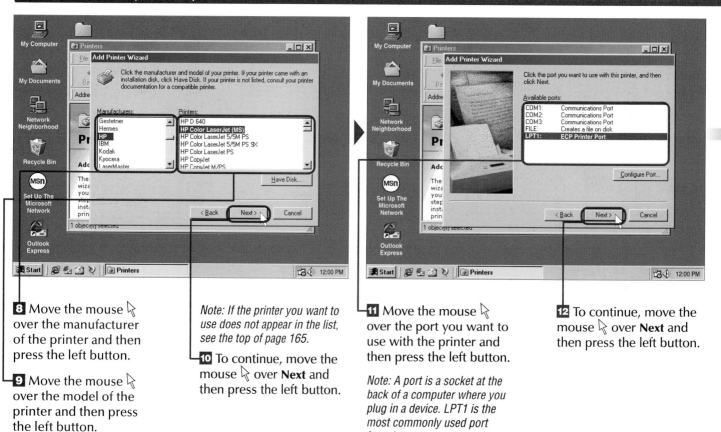

8 Move the mouse ⬚ over the manufacturer of the printer and then press the left button.

9 Move the mouse ⬚ over the model of the printer and then press the left button.

Note: If the printer you want to use does not appear in the list, see the top of page 165.

10 To continue, move the mouse ⬚ over **Next** and then press the left button.

11 Move the mouse ⬚ over the port you want to use with the printer and then press the left button.

Note: A port is a socket at the back of a computer where you plug in a device. LPT1 is the most commonly used port for printers.

12 To continue, move the mouse ⬚ over **Next** and then press the left button.

What if the printer I want to install does not appear in the list?

If the printer you want to install does not appear in the list, you can use the installation disk(s) that came with the printer.

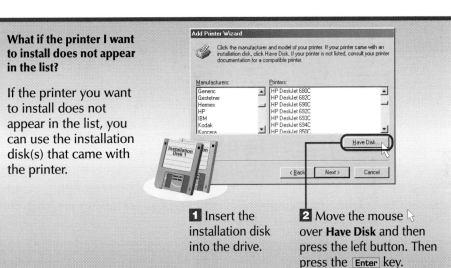

1 Insert the installation disk into the drive.

2 Move the mouse over **Have Disk** and then press the left button. Then press the `Enter` key.

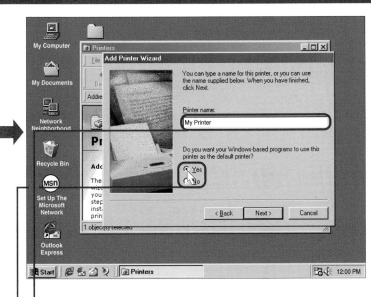

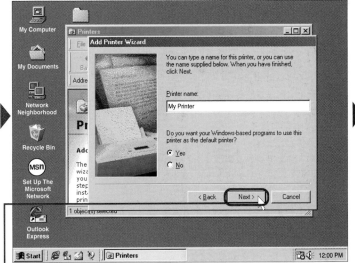

13 Windows provides a name for the printer. To use a different name, type the name.

14 To specify if you want to use the printer as the default printer, move the mouse over one of these options and then press the left button (○ changes to ⊙).

Yes
Files will always print to this printer.

No
Files will print to this printer only when you select the printer.

15 To continue, move the mouse over **Next** and then press the left button.

CONTINUED➡

INSTALL A PRINTER (CONTINUED)

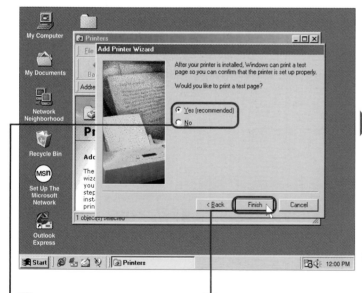

16 To specify if you want to print a test page, move the mouse ⍉ over **Yes** or **No** and then press the left button (○ changes to ⊙).

17 To install the printer, move the mouse ⍉ over **Finish** and then press the left button.

■ The Insert Disk dialog box appears, asking you to insert the Windows 98 CD-ROM disc.

18 Insert the CD-ROM disc into the drive.

19 To continue, move the mouse ⍉ over **OK** and then press the left button.

■ Windows copies the necessary files to your computer.

Why do I need the Windows 98 CD-ROM disc to install a printer?

Your computer needs special software, called a driver, to be able to use a new printer. A driver is a program that allows your computer to communicate with the printer. The Windows 98 CD-ROM disc includes the most popular drivers.

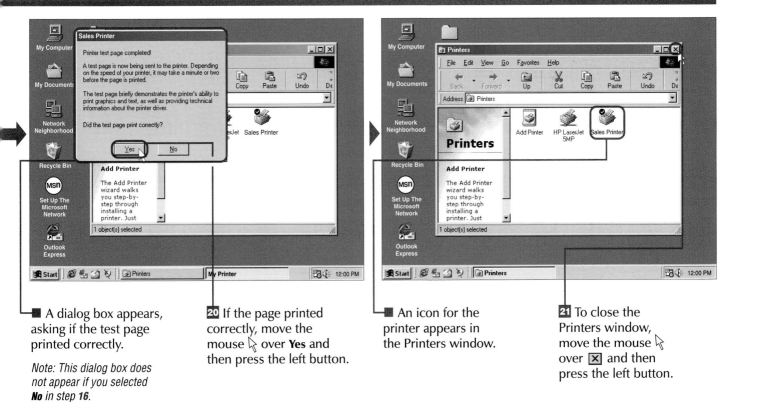

■ A dialog box appears, asking if the test page printed correctly.

*Note: This dialog box does not appear if you selected **No** in step 16.*

20 If the page printed correctly, move the mouse ⬡ over **Yes** and then press the left button.

■ An icon for the printer appears in the Printers window.

21 To close the Printers window, move the mouse ⬡ over ⊠ and then press the left button.

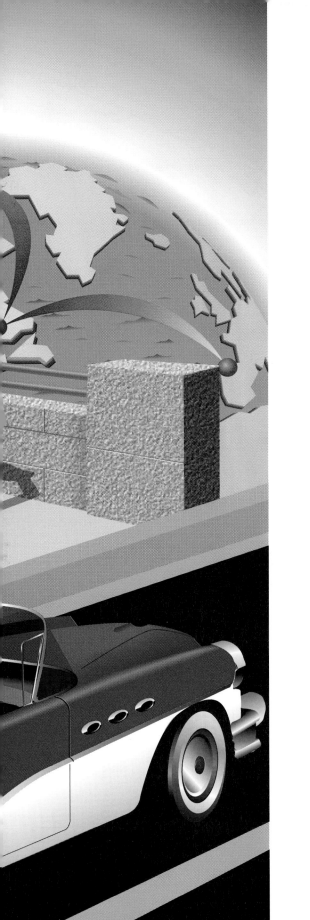

CHAPTER 9

BROWSE THE WEB

What is the Web? This chapter will explain how the Web works and how you can use it to transfer information to your computer from sites around the world.

The World Wide Web is part of the Internet, which is the largest computer system in the world. The Web consists of a huge collection of documents stored on hundreds of thousands of computers.

Web Pages

A Web page is a document on the Web. You can find Web pages on every subject imaginable. There are Web pages that offer information such as newspaper and magazine articles, movie clips, recipes, Shakespearean plays, airline schedules and more. You can also purchase items, do your banking and get programs and games on the Web.

Web Sites

A Web site is a collection of Web pages maintained by a college, university, government agency, company or individual.

URLs

Each Web page has a unique address, called a Uniform Resource Locator (URL). You can display any Web page if you know its URL. Most Web page URLs start with http (HyperText Transfer Protocol).

Links

Web pages contain highlighted text or images, called links, that are connected to other pages on the Web. You can select a link on a Web page to display another page located on the same computer or on a computer across the city, country or world.

Links allow you to easily move through a vast amount of information by jumping from one Web page to another. This is known as "browsing the Web."

Connecting to the Internet

Most people use an Internet Service Provider (ISP) to connect to the Internet. Once you pay your service provider to connect to the Internet, you can exchange information on the Internet free of charge.

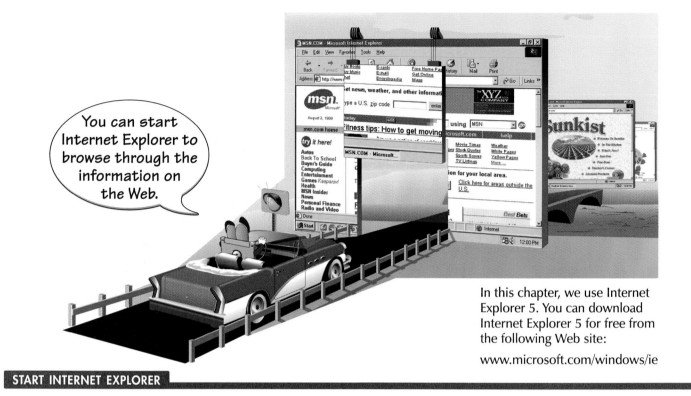

You can start Internet Explorer to browse through the information on the Web.

In this chapter, we use Internet Explorer 5. You can download Internet Explorer 5 for free from the following Web site:

www.microsoft.com/windows/ie

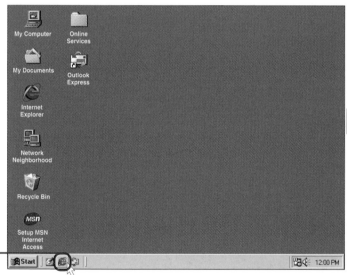

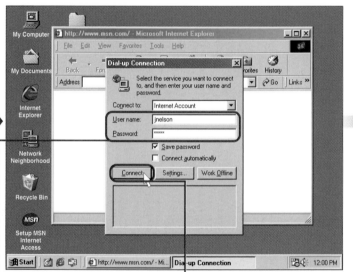

1 To start Internet Explorer so you can begin browsing the Web, move the mouse over 🍵 and then press the left button.

Note: If the Internet Connection Wizard appears, see the top of page 173.

■ The Dial-up Connection dialog box appears.

■ This area displays your user name and password.

Note: A symbol (x) appears for each character in your password to prevent others from viewing the password.

2 To connect to your Internet service provider, move the mouse over **Connect** and then press the left button.

Why does the Internet Connection Wizard appear when I try to start Internet Explorer?

The Internet Connection Wizard appears the first time you start Internet Explorer to help you get connected to the Internet. You can use the wizard to set up a new connection to the Internet or to set up an existing account. To set up an existing account, ask your Internet service provider for the information you need to enter.

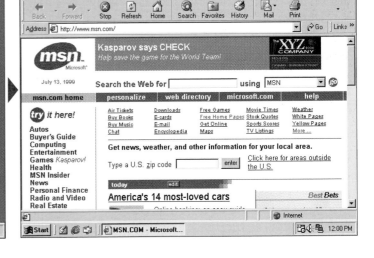

■ The Microsoft Internet Explorer window appears, displaying your home page.

Note: A different Web page may appear on your screen.

3 To maximize the window to fill your screen, move the mouse ♀ over ▢ and then press the left button.

■ The window maximizes to fill your screen.

You can easily display a page on the Web that you have heard or read about.

You need to know the address of the Web page you want to view. Each page on the Web has a unique address, called a Uniform Resource Locator (URL).

URL

http://www.flowerstop.com

DISPLAY A SPECIFIC WEB PAGE

1 To highlight the current Web page address, move the mouse I over this area and then press the left button.

2 Type the address of the Web page you want to view and then press the Enter key.

How can I save time when typing Web page addresses?

You can leave off **http://** when typing a Web page address. For example, you could type **http://www.maran.com** or **www.maran.com** to display the maranGraphics Web page.

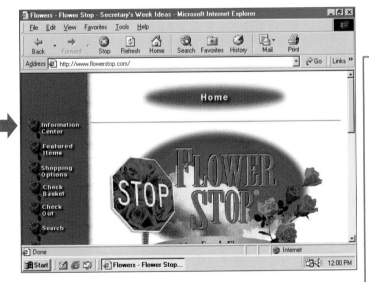

■ The Web page appears on your screen.

Internet Explorer remembers the addresses of Web pages you recently visited. You can select one of these addresses to quickly display a Web page.

■ When you begin typing the address of a Web page you previously visited, a list of matching addresses appears.

1 Move the mouse ⬥ over the address of the Web page you want to display and then press the left button.

> A link connects text or a picture on one Web page to another Web page. When you select the text or picture, the other Web page appears.

SELECT A LINK

1 Move the mouse ⬚ over a highlighted word or picture of interest and then press the left button.

■ The mouse ⬚ changes to a hand (🖑) when over a link.

■ The Web page connected to the word or picture appears.

■ This area displays the name of the Web page.

■ This icon is animated as the Web page transfers to your computer.

■ This area displays the address of the Web page.

You can refresh a Web page to update the displayed information, such as the current news. Internet Explorer will transfer a fresh copy of the Web page to your computer.

REFRESH A WEB PAGE

1 To transfer a fresh copy of the displayed Web page to your computer, move the mouse ⌖ over **Refresh** and then press the left button.

■ A fresh copy of the Web page appears on your screen.

If a Web page is taking a long time to appear on your screen, you can stop transferring the page and try connecting again later.

The best time to try connecting to a Web site is during off-peak hours, such as nights and weekends, when fewer people are using the Internet.

STOP TRANSFER OF INFORMATION

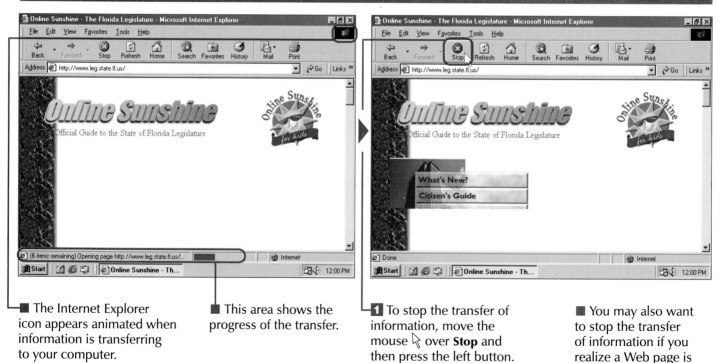

■ The Internet Explorer icon appears animated when information is transferring to your computer.

■ This area shows the progress of the transfer.

1 To stop the transfer of information, move the mouse ↖ over **Stop** and then press the left button.

■ You may also want to stop the transfer of information if you realize a Web page is of no interest to you.

You can easily move back and forth through Web pages you have viewed since you last started Internet Explorer.

MOVE THROUGH WEB PAGES

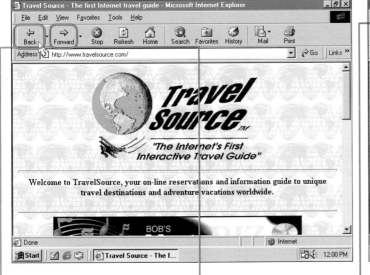

1 To display the last Web page you viewed, move the mouse ⟲ over **Back** and then press the left button.

■ To move forward through the Web pages you have viewed, move the mouse ⟲ over **Forward** and then press the left button.

You can display a list of the Web pages you have viewed.

1 To display a list of Web pages you have viewed, move the mouse ⟲ over ⬇ beside **Back** or **Forward** and then press the left button.

2 Move the mouse ⟲ over the Web page you want to view and then press the left button.

You can specify which Web page you want to appear each time you start Internet Explorer. This page is called your home page.

DISPLAY AND CHANGE YOUR HOME PAGE

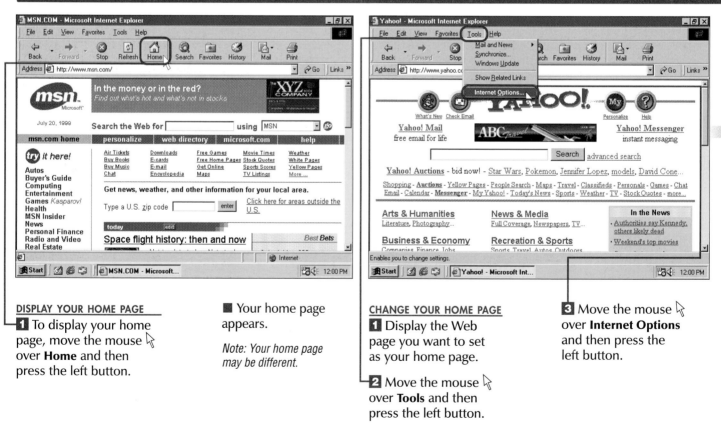

DISPLAY YOUR HOME PAGE

1 To display your home page, move the mouse �}over **Home** and then press the left button.

■ Your home page appears.

Note: Your home page may be different.

CHANGE YOUR HOME PAGE

1 Display the Web page you want to set as your home page.

2 Move the mouse �}over **Tools** and then press the left button.

3 Move the mouse �}over **Internet Options** and then press the left button.

Which Web page should I use as my home page?

You can choose any page on the Web as your home page. You may want to choose a page that provides a good starting point for exploring the Web. Your home page can also be a favorite Web page.

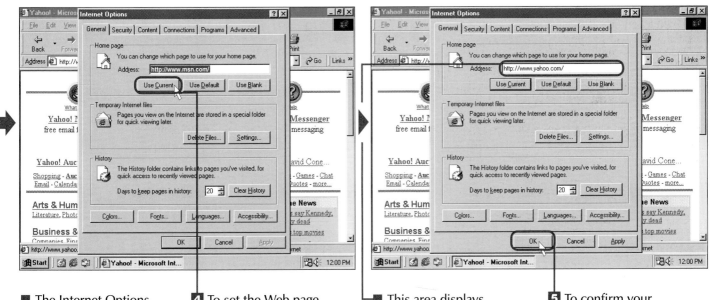

■ The Internet Options dialog box appears.

4 To set the Web page displayed on your screen as your new home page, move the mouse ⃗ over **Use Current** and then press the left button.

■ This area displays the address of the new home page.

5 To confirm your change, move the mouse ⃗ over **OK** and then press the left button.

You can use the Favorites feature to create a list of Web pages you frequently visit. You can quickly return to any Web page in the list.

ADD A WEB PAGE TO FAVORITES

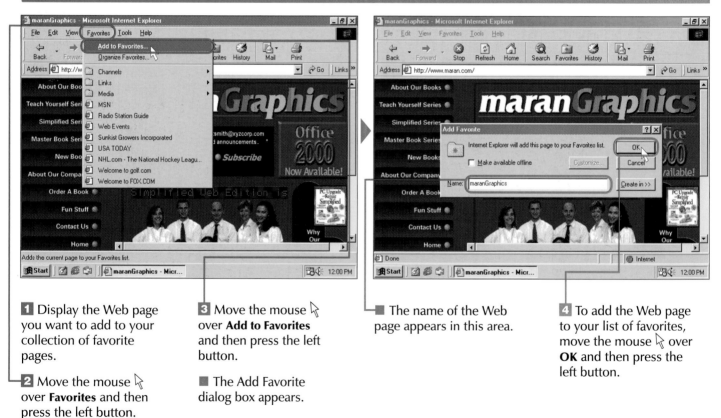

1 Display the Web page you want to add to your collection of favorite pages.

2 Move the mouse ⟋ over **Favorites** and then press the left button.

3 Move the mouse ⟋ over **Add to Favorites** and then press the left button.

■ The Add Favorite dialog box appears.

■ The name of the Web page appears in this area.

4 To add the Web page to your list of favorites, move the mouse ⟋ over **OK** and then press the left button.

What are the benefits of adding a Web page to my list of favorites?

Web page addresses can be long and complex. Selecting Web pages from your list of favorites saves you from having to remember and constantly retype the same addresses over and over again.

VIEW A FAVORITE WEB PAGE

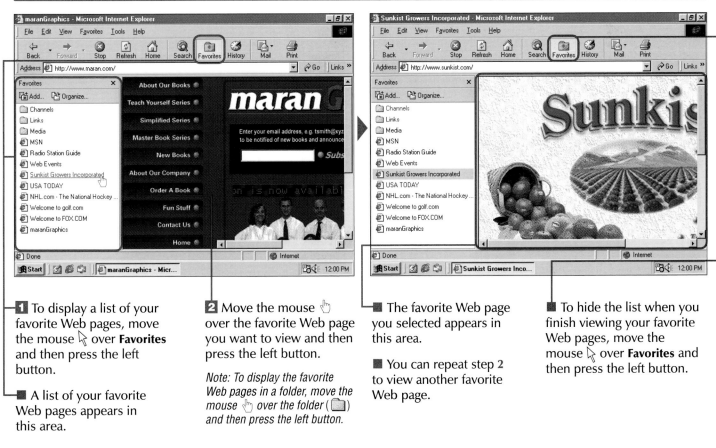

1 To display a list of your favorite Web pages, move the mouse ⟦ over **Favorites** and then press the left button.

■ A list of your favorite Web pages appears in this area.

2 Move the mouse ⟦ over the favorite Web page you want to view and then press the left button.

Note: To display the favorite Web pages in a folder, move the mouse ⟦ over the folder (📁) and then press the left button.

■ The favorite Web page you selected appears in this area.

■ You can repeat step **2** to view another favorite Web page.

■ To hide the list when you finish viewing your favorite Web pages, move the mouse ⟦ over **Favorites** and then press the left button.

DISPLAY HISTORY OF VIEWED WEB PAGES

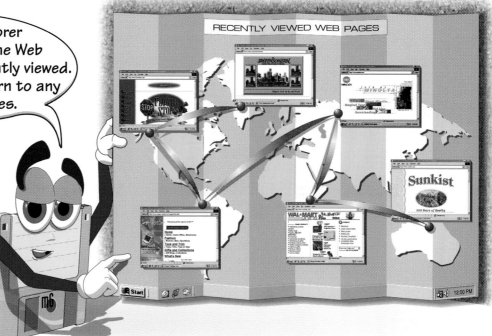

Internet Explorer keeps track of the Web pages you have recently viewed. You can easily return to any of these pages.

RECENTLY VIEWED WEB PAGES

DISPLAY HISTORY OF VIEWED WEB PAGES

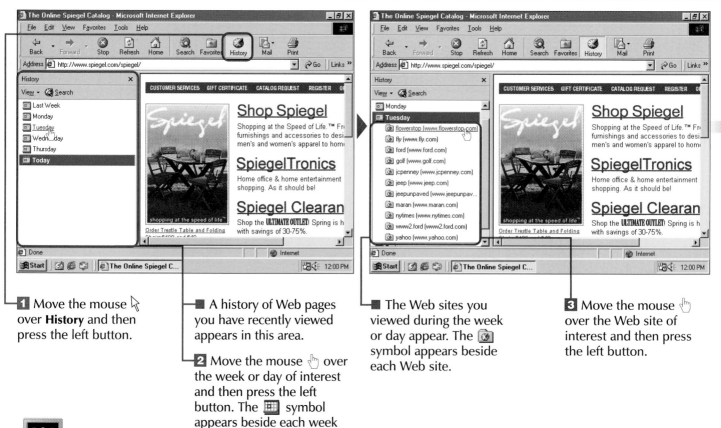

1 Move the mouse ⟶ over **History** and then press the left button.

■ A history of Web pages you have recently viewed appears in this area.

2 Move the mouse 🖑 over the week or day of interest and then press the left button. The 🔲 symbol appears beside each week and day.

■ The Web sites you viewed during the week or day appear. The 🔘 symbol appears beside each Web site.

3 Move the mouse 🖑 over the Web site of interest and then press the left button.

How long does Internet Explorer keep track of the Web pages I have viewed?

Internet Explorer keeps track of the Web pages you have viewed during the last 20 days.

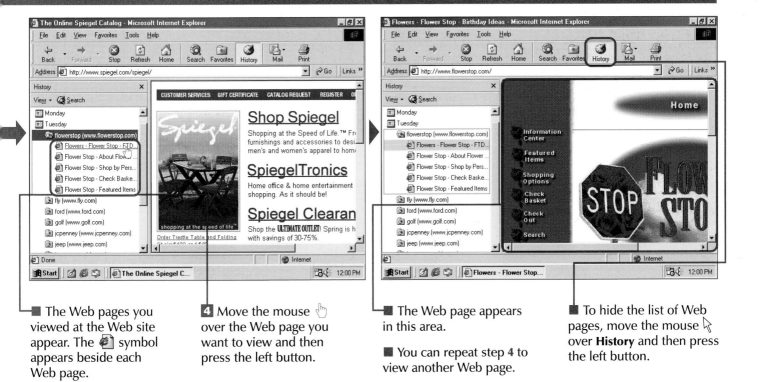

■ The Web pages you viewed at the Web site appear. The 🗐 symbol appears beside each Web page.

4 Move the mouse 🖑 over the Web page you want to view and then press the left button.

■ The Web page appears in this area.

■ You can repeat step **4** to view another Web page.

■ To hide the list of Web pages, move the mouse ▷ over **History** and then press the left button.

You can find pages on the Web that discuss topics of interest to you.

There are search tools available on the Web that catalog information about millions of Web pages. Popular search tools include Excite, Yahoo! and Lycos.

SEARCH THE WEB

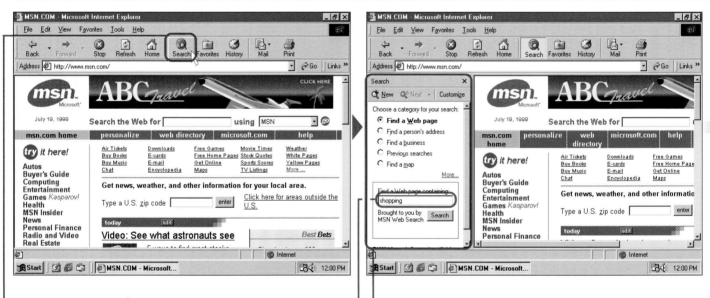

1 Move the mouse ↘ over **Search** and then press the left button.

*Note: The Security Warning dialog box may appear if Microsoft needs to transfer information to your computer. To transfer the information, move the mouse ↘ over **Yes** and then press the left button.*

■ The search area appears, displaying a tool you can use to search for information on the Web.

2 Move the mouse I over this area and then press the left button. Then type a word you want to search for.

3 Press the Enter key to start the search.

How do search tools find Web pages?

Some search tools use a program, called a robot, to scan the Web for new and updated pages. Thousands of new Web pages are located and cataloged by robots every day. New pages are also cataloged when people submit information about the pages they have created.

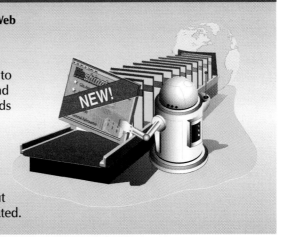

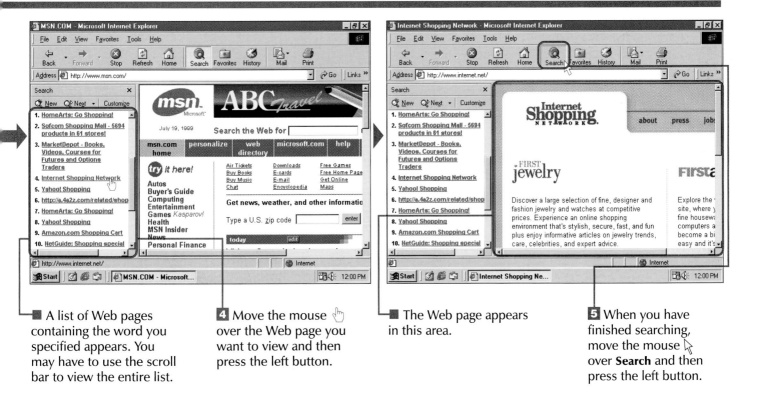

■ A list of Web pages containing the word you specified appears. You may have to use the scroll bar to view the entire list.

4 Move the mouse 🖑 over the Web page you want to view and then press the left button.

■ The Web page appears in this area.

5 When you have finished searching, move the mouse ☒ over **Search** and then press the left button.

You can set up one computer on a network to share its Internet connection with other computers on the network.

Sharing an Internet connection allows several computers to access the Internet at the same time using one modem or high-speed connection.

SET UP THE COMPUTER CONNECTED TO THE INTERNET

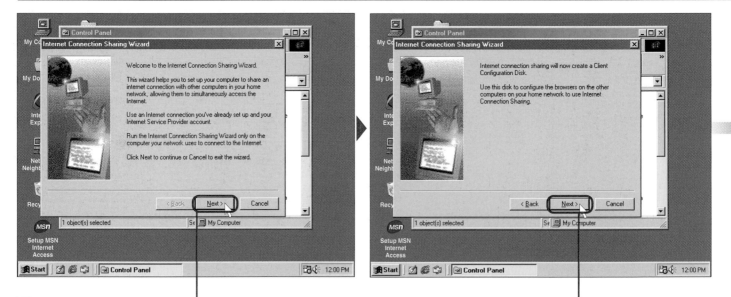

1 Install the Internet Connection Sharing component on the computer connected to the Internet. To install a component, see page 158.

Note: The Internet Connection Sharing component is found in the Internet Tools category.

■ The Internet Connection Sharing Wizard appears.

2 To set up the computer to share its Internet connection, move the mouse ⟍ over **Next** and then press the left button.

■ The wizard will create a floppy disk that allows you to set up other computers on the network.

3 To continue, move the mouse ⟍ over **Next** and then press the left button.

Does each computer that will share the Internet connection have to use Windows 98?

The computer connected to the Internet must use Windows 98 Second Edition. The other computers on the network can use Windows 95, Windows 98 or Windows NT.

Each computer on the network must have the TCP/IP network protocol installed. A protocol is a language that computers and other devices on a network use to communicate. For more information, see the Windows Help feature.

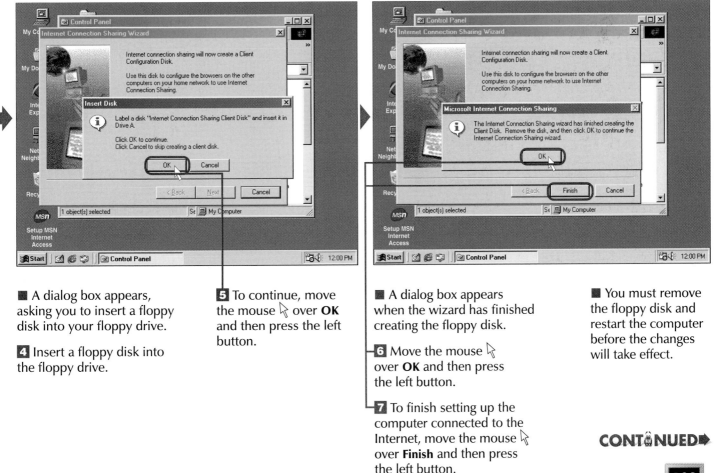

■ A dialog box appears, asking you to insert a floppy disk into your floppy drive.

4 Insert a floppy disk into the floppy drive.

5 To continue, move the mouse ⌖ over **OK** and then press the left button.

■ A dialog box appears when the wizard has finished creating the floppy disk.

6 Move the mouse ⌖ over **OK** and then press the left button.

7 To finish setting up the computer connected to the Internet, move the mouse ⌖ over **Finish** and then press the left button.

■ You must remove the floppy disk and restart the computer before the changes will take effect.

CONTINUED➡

After you set up the computer connected to the Internet, you can set up other computers on the network to use the shared connection.

You will need the floppy disk the wizard created on page 189.

SET UP A COMPUTER TO USE A SHARED INTERNET CONNECTION

1 Insert the floppy disk the wizard created on page 189 into the floppy drive of a computer you want to use the shared Internet connection.

2 Move the mouse over **My Computer** and then quickly press the left button twice.

3 Move the mouse over the floppy drive and then quickly press the left button twice.

4 Move the mouse over **icsclset** and then quickly press the left button twice.

■ The Browser Connection Setup Wizard appears.

5 To continue, move the mouse over **Next** and then press the left button.

What must I do before setting up a computer to use a shared Internet connection?

Before you set up a computer to use a shared Internet connection, you must make sure the computer with the Internet connection is turned on and connected to both the Internet and the network.

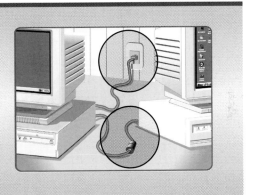

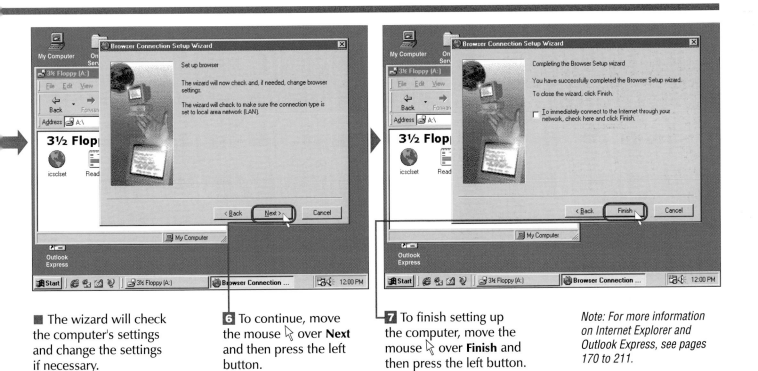

■ The wizard will check the computer's settings and change the settings if necessary.

6 To continue, move the mouse ⤢ over **Next** and then press the left button.

7 To finish setting up the computer, move the mouse ⤢ over **Finish** and then press the left button.

■ When you start Internet Explorer or Outlook Express on this computer, the computer will use the shared Internet connection to access the Internet.

Note: For more information on Internet Explorer and Outlook Express, see pages 170 to 211.

CHAPTER 10

EXCHANGE ELECTRONIC MAIL

Would you like to exchange electronic mail messages with friends and colleagues around the world? Find out how in this chapter.

You can exchange electronic mail (e-mail) with people around the world.

E-mail provides a fast, economical and convenient way to send messages to family, friends and colleagues.

COST

Once you pay a service provider for a connection to the Internet, there is no charge for sending and receiving e-mail. You do not have to pay extra if you send a long message or the message travels around the world.

Exchanging e-mail can save you money on long-distance calls. The next time you are about to pick up the telephone, consider sending an e-mail message instead.

CONVENIENCE

You can create and send e-mail messages at any time. Unlike telephone calls, the person receiving the message does not have to be at the computer when you send the message. E-mail makes communicating with people in different time zones very convenient.

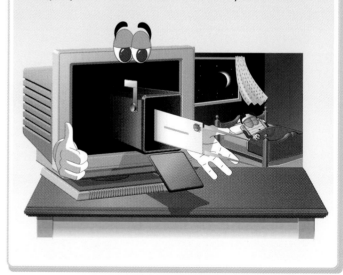

PARTS OF AN E-MAIL ADDRESS

You can send a message to anyone around the world if you know the person's e-mail address. An e-mail address defines the location of an individual's mailbox on the Internet.

An e-mail address consists of two parts separated by the @ ("at") symbol. An e-mail address cannot contain spaces.

mvickers@abc.com

■ The **user name** is the name of the person's account. This can be a real name or a nickname.

■ The **domain name** is the location of the person's account on the Internet. Periods (.) separate the various parts of the domain name.

COMPOSING AN E-MAIL MESSAGE

Smileys

You can use special characters, called smileys or emoticons, to express emotions in e-mail messages. These characters resemble human faces if you turn them sideways.

Cry	:'-(
Frown	:-(
Indifferent	:-I
Laugh	:-D

| Smile | :-) |
| Surprise | :-0 |

Wink

Shouting

A MESSAGE WRITTEN IN CAPITAL LETTERS IS ANNOYING AND HARD TO READ. THIS IS CALLED SHOUTING. Always use upper and lower case letters when typing e-mail messages.

HOW ARE YOU?

You can start Outlook Express to exchange e-mail messages with people around the world.

In this chapter, we use Outlook Express 5, which is part of Internet Explorer 5. You can download Internet Explorer 5 from the following Web site:

www.microsoft.com/windows/ie

START OUTLOOK EXPRESS

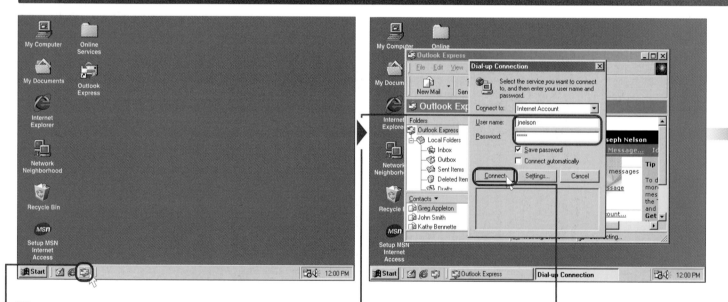

1 To start Outlook Express, move the mouse ⌖ over [icon] and then press the left button.

Note: If the Internet Connection Wizard appears, see the top of page 173.

■ The Dial-up Connection dialog box appears.

■ This area displays your user name and password.

Note: A symbol (×) appears for each character in your password to prevent others from viewing the password.

2 To connect to your Internet service provider, move the mouse ⌖ over **Connect** and then press the left button.

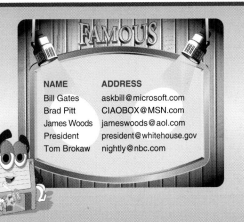

Can I use Outlook Express to e-mail famous people?

You can send a message to anyone if you know the person's e-mail address. Here are some e-mail addresses of famous people.

NAME	ADDRESS
Bill Gates	askbill@microsoft.com
Brad Pitt	CIAOBOX@MSN.com
James Woods	jameswoods@aol.com
President	president@whitehouse.gov
Tom Brokaw	nightly@nbc.com

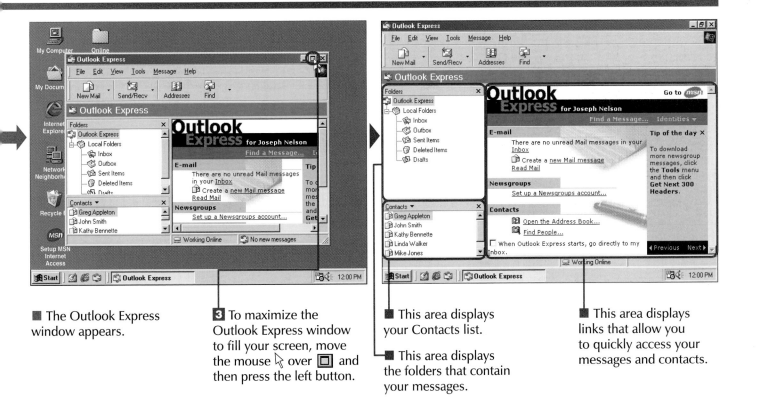

■ The Outlook Express window appears.

3 To maximize the Outlook Express window to fill your screen, move the mouse over ▢ and then press the left button.

■ This area displays your Contacts list.

■ This area displays the folders that contain your messages.

■ This area displays links that allow you to quickly access your messages and contacts.

You can easily open your messages to read their contents.

READ MESSAGES

1 Move the mouse over the folder containing the messages you want to read and then press the left button. The folder is highlighted.

■ The number in brackets beside the folder indicates how many unread messages the folder contains. The number disappears when you have read all the messages in the folder.

■ This area displays the messages in the highlighted folder. Messages you have not read display a closed envelope (✉) and appear in **bold** type.

■ A paper clip icon (📎) appears beside a message with an attached file.

What folders does Outlook Express use to store my messages?

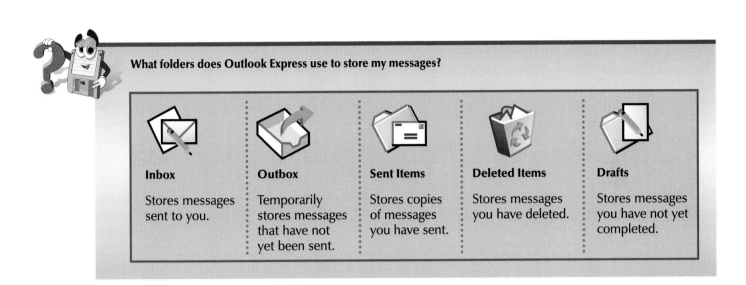

Inbox
Stores messages sent to you.

Outbox
Temporarily stores messages that have not yet been sent.

Sent Items
Stores copies of messages you have sent.

Deleted Items
Stores messages you have deleted.

Drafts
Stores messages you have not yet completed.

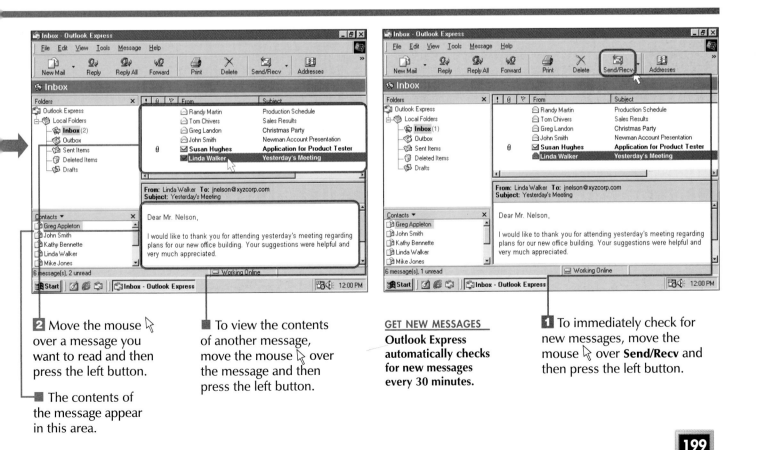

■2 Move the mouse ⟍ over a message you want to read and then press the left button.

■ The contents of the message appear in this area.

■ To view the contents of another message, move the mouse ⟍ over the message and then press the left button.

GET NEW MESSAGES
Outlook Express automatically checks for new messages every 30 minutes.

■1 To immediately check for new messages, move the mouse ⟍ over **Send/Recv** and then press the left button.

You can send a message to exchange ideas or request information.

COMPOSE A MESSAGE

1 Move the mouse ⊮ over **New Mail** and then press the left button.

■ The New Message window appears.

2 Type the e-mail address of the person you want to receive the message.

Note: To select a name from the address book, see page 204. Then skip to step 4.

3 To send a copy of the message to another person, move the mouse I over this area and then press the left button. Then type the e-mail address.

Note: For information on sending copies, see the top of page 205.

How can I quickly send a message to a person in my Contacts list?

To quickly send a message to a person in your Contacts list, move the mouse ⬧ over the name of the person in the Contacts list and then quickly press the left button twice. Then perform steps **3** to **6** below.

For more information on the Contacts List, see the top of page 203.

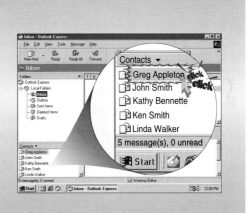

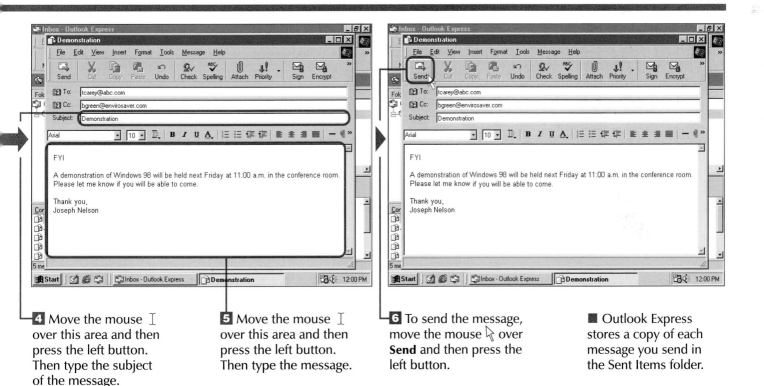

4 Move the mouse I over this area and then press the left button. Then type the subject of the message.

5 Move the mouse I over this area and then press the left button. Then type the message.

6 To send the message, move the mouse ⬧ over **Send** and then press the left button.

■ Outlook Express stores a copy of each message you send in the Sent Items folder.

You can use the address book to store the e-mail addresses of people you frequently send messages to.

ADD A NAME TO THE ADDRESS BOOK

1 Move the mouse ⌖ over **Addresses** and then press the left button.

■ The Address Book window appears.

2 Move the mouse ⌖ over **New** and then press the left button.

3 To add a name to the address book, move the mouse ⌖ over **New Contact** and then press the left button.

■ The Properties dialog box appears.

Is there another way to add a name to my address book?

Each time you reply to a message, the author's name and e-mail address are automatically added to your address book. Outlook Express also adds the name to the Contacts list at the bottom of the Outlook Express window.

For information on using the Contacts list to send a message, see the top of page 201.

To: tjones@abc.com

4 Type the first name of the person you want to add.

5 Move the mouse I over this area and then press the left button. Then type the last name.

6 Move the mouse I over this area and then press the left button. Then type the e-mail address.

7 Move the mouse ⫯ over **OK** and then press the left button.

■ The name appears in the Address Book window.

8 To close the Address Book window, move the mouse ⫯ over ⊠ and then press the left button.

When sending a message, you can select the name of the person you want to receive the message from the address book.

Selecting names from the address book saves you from having to remember e-mail addresses you often use.

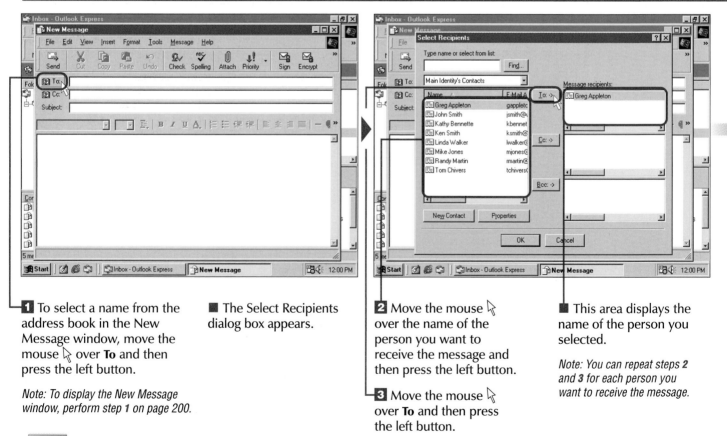

1 To select a name from the address book in the New Message window, move the mouse Ⓚ over **To** and then press the left button.

Note: To display the New Message window, perform step 1 on page 200.

■ The Select Recipients dialog box appears.

2 Move the mouse ⓀⓀ over the name of the person you want to receive the message and then press the left button.

3 Move the mouse ⓀⓀ over **To** and then press the left button.

■ This area displays the name of the person you selected.

Note: You can repeat steps 2 and 3 for each person you want to receive the message.

How can I address a message I want to send?

To

Sends the message to the person you specify.

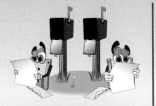

Carbon Copy (Cc)

Sends an exact copy of the message to a person who is not directly involved, but would be interested in the message.

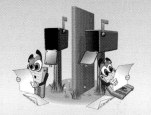

Blind Carbon Copy (Bcc)

Sends an exact copy of the message to a person without anyone else knowing that the person received the message.

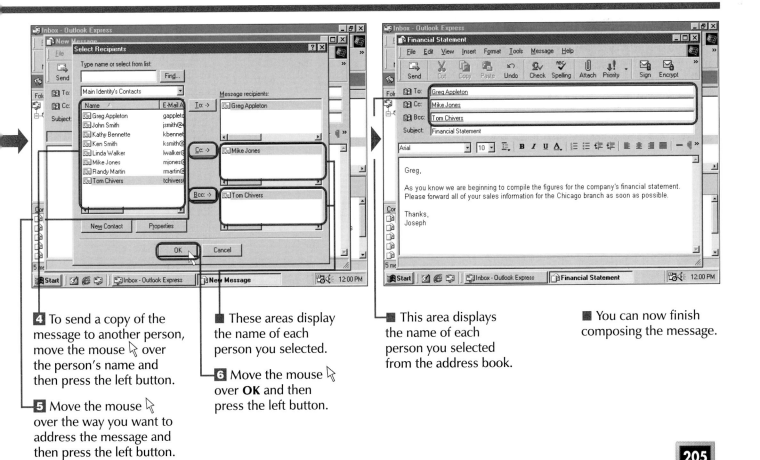

4 To send a copy of the message to another person, move the mouse ⟲ over the person's name and then press the left button.

5 Move the mouse ⟲ over the way you want to address the message and then press the left button.

■ These areas display the name of each person you selected.

6 Move the mouse ⟲ over **OK** and then press the left button.

■ This area displays the name of each person you selected from the address book.

■ You can now finish composing the message.

You can attach a file to a message you are sending. Attaching a file is useful when you want to include additional information with a message.

ATTACH A FILE TO A MESSAGE

1 To compose a message, perform steps **1** to **5** starting on page 200.

2 To attach a file to the message, move the mouse ⬚ over **Attach** and then press the left button.

■ The Insert Attachment dialog box appears.

■ This area shows the location of the displayed files.

3 Move the mouse ⬚ over the name of the file you want to attach to the message and then press the left button.

4 Move the mouse ⬚ over **Attach** and then press the left button.

What types of files can I attach to a message?

You can attach files such as documents, pictures, programs, sounds and videos to a message. The computer receiving the message must have the necessary hardware and software to display or play the file.

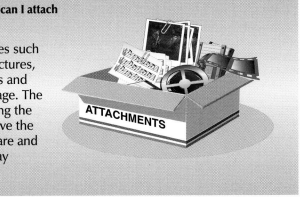

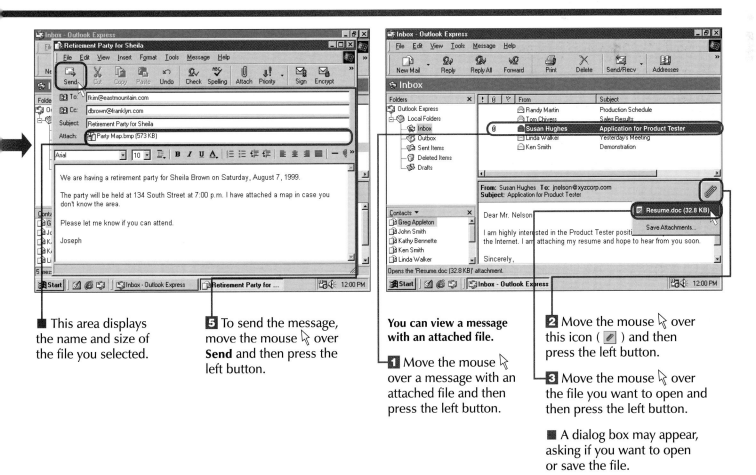

■ This area displays the name and size of the file you selected.

5 To send the message, move the mouse ⇧ over **Send** and then press the left button.

You can view a message with an attached file.

1 Move the mouse ⇧ over a message with an attached file and then press the left button.

2 Move the mouse ⇧ over this icon (📎) and then press the left button.

3 Move the mouse ⇧ over the file you want to open and then press the left button.

■ A dialog box may appear, asking if you want to open or save the file.

REPLY TO A MESSAGE

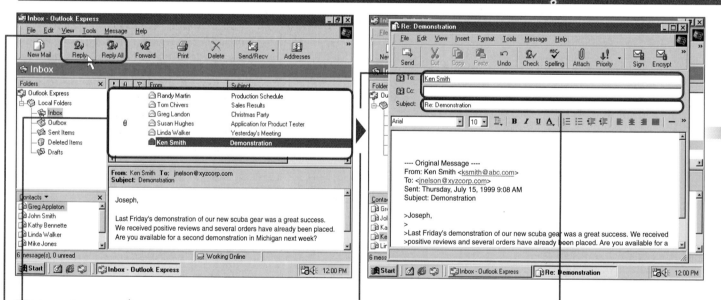

1 Move the mouse ⌖ over the message you want to reply to and then press the left button.

2 Move the mouse ⌖ over the reply option you want to use and then press the left button.

Reply
Sends a reply to the author only.

Reply All
Sends a reply to the author and everyone who received the original message.

■ A window appears for you to compose the message.

■ Outlook Express fills in the e-mail address(es) for you.

■ Outlook Express also fills in the subject, starting the subject with **Re:**

How can I save time when typing a message?

Abbreviations are commonly used to save time when typing a message.

Abbreviation	Meaning
BTW	by the way
FAQ	frequently asked questions
FOAF	friend of a friend
FWIW	for what it's worth
FYI	for your information

Abbreviation	Meaning
IMO	in my opinion
L8R	later
LOL	laughing out loud
ROTFL	rolling on the floor laughing
WRT	with respect to

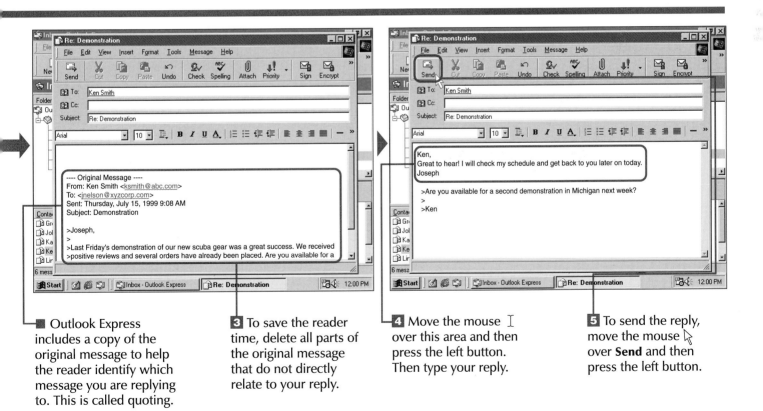

■ Outlook Express includes a copy of the original message to help the reader identify which message you are replying to. This is called quoting.

3 To save the reader time, delete all parts of the original message that do not directly relate to your reply.

4 Move the mouse I over this area and then press the left button. Then type your reply.

5 To send the reply, move the mouse ▷ over **Send** and then press the left button.

After reading a message, you can add comments and then forward the message to a friend or colleague.

FORWARD A MESSAGE

1 Move the mouse ⍾ over the message you want to forward and then press the left button.

2 Move the mouse ⍾ over **Forward** and then press the left button.

■ A window appears, displaying the message you are forwarding.

3 Type the e-mail address of the person you want to receive the message.

Note: To select a name from the address book, see page 204.

■ Outlook Express fills in the subject for you, starting the subject with **Fw:**

4 Move the mouse I over this area and then press the left button. Then type any comments about the message you are forwarding.

5 To forward the message, move the mouse ⍾ over **Send** and then press the left button.

DELETE A MESSAGE

You can delete a message you no longer need. Deleting messages prevents your folders from becoming cluttered with messages.

DELETE A MESSAGE

1 Move the mouse ⟍ over the message you want to delete and then press the left button.

2 Press the Delete key.

◼ Outlook Express removes the message from the current folder and places the message in the Deleted Items folder.

Note: Deleting a message from the Deleted Items folder will permanently remove the message from your computer.

CHAPTER 11

WORK WITH CHANNELS

What are channels and how do I work with them? In this chapter you will learn how these specially designed Web sites can deliver Web content to your desktop.

A channel is a Web site that automatically delivers information from the Internet to your computer. You can add a channel of interest.

If you are using Windows 98 Second Edition, you may not have access to channels.

ADD A CHANNEL

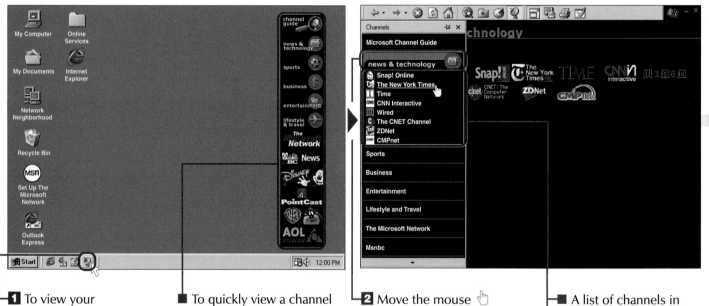

1 To view your channels, move the mouse ⟨ over 🔍 and then press the left button.

■ To quickly view a channel displayed on the Channel Bar, move the mouse ⟨ over the channel and then press the left button.

Note: If the Channel Bar is not on your desktop, you may not have access to channels or the Channel Bar may be hidden. To display a hidden Channel Bar, see page 220.

2 Move the mouse ⟨ᵐ⟩ over a category of interest and then press the left button.

■ A list of channels in the category appears.

3 Move the mouse ⟨ᵐ⟩ over a channel of interest and then press the left button.

Why do my screens look different than the screens shown below?

If you upgraded to Windows 98 Second Edition or Internet Explorer 5, an Internet Explorer window appears when you perform step **1**. You can perform steps **2** to **4** in the Internet Explorer window. The Offline Favorite Wizard will then appear, to help you add the channel.

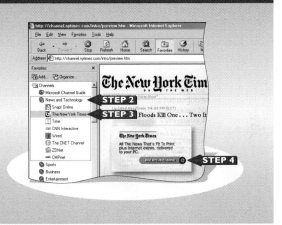

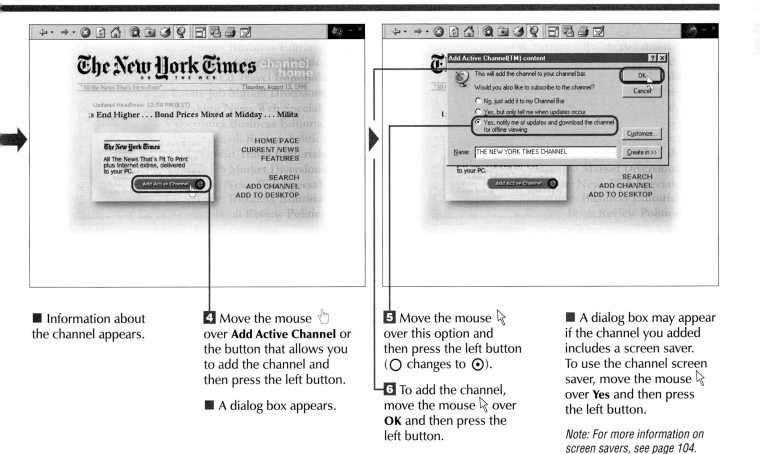

■ Information about the channel appears.

4 Move the mouse over **Add Active Channel** or the button that allows you to add the channel and then press the left button.

■ A dialog box appears.

5 Move the mouse over this option and then press the left button (○ changes to ⊙).

6 To add the channel, move the mouse over **OK** and then press the left button.

■ A dialog box may appear if the channel you added includes a screen saver. To use the channel screen saver, move the mouse over **Yes** and then press the left button.

Note: For more information on screen savers, see page 104.

You can add active content from the Web to your desktop. Active content is information that changes on your screen, such as a stock ticker or a weather map.

ADD AN ACTIVE DESKTOP ITEM

1 Move the mouse over a blank area on your desktop and then press the **right** button. A menu appears.

2 Move the mouse over **Properties** and then press the left button.

■ The Display Properties dialog box appears.

3 Move the mouse over the **Web** tab and then press the left button.

4 This option must display a check mark (☑) to add Active Desktop items. To add a check mark, move the mouse over this option and then press the left button.

What types of items can I add to my desktop?

There are many interesting Active Desktop items available. For example, you can personalize your desktop with a comic strip or with a news ticker displaying up-to-the-minute headlines. Some Active Desktop items contain sounds or videos.

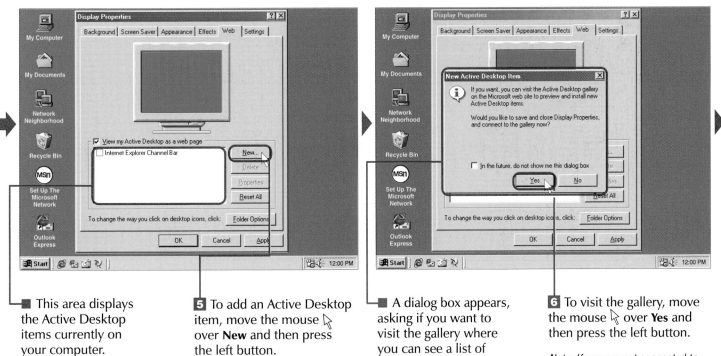

■ This area displays the Active Desktop items currently on your computer.

5 To add an Active Desktop item, move the mouse ⬚ over **New** and then press the left button.

■ A dialog box appears, asking if you want to visit the gallery where you can see a list of Active Desktop items.

6 To visit the gallery, move the mouse ⬚ over **Yes** and then press the left button.

Note: If you are not connected to the Internet, a dialog box may appear that allows you to connect.

CONTINUED➡

The gallery offers various items you can add to your desktop. The items are organized into categories such as news, sports, entertainment and travel.

ADD AN ACTIVE DESKTOP ITEM (CONTINUED)

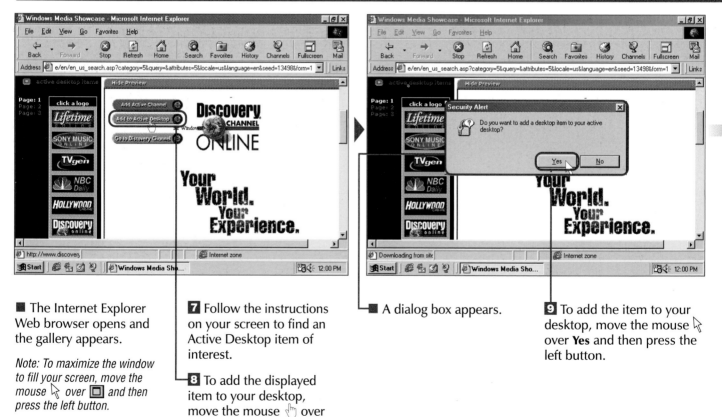

■ The Internet Explorer Web browser opens and the gallery appears.

Note: To maximize the window to fill your screen, move the mouse � over ▢ and then press the left button.

7 Follow the instructions on your screen to find an Active Desktop item of interest.

8 To add the displayed item to your desktop, move the mouse ☜ over **Add to Active Desktop** and then press the left button.

■ A dialog box appears.

9 To add the item to your desktop, move the mouse � over **Yes** and then press the left button.

Why does the gallery look different on my computer?

Companies, organizations and individuals constantly make changes to their Web pages to update information and improve their Web sites. The Web page shown on your screen may look different from the Web page shown in this book.

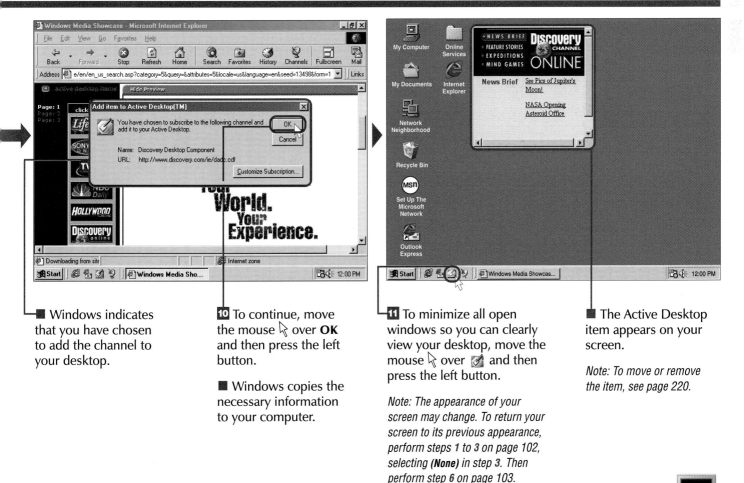

■ Windows indicates that you have chosen to add the channel to your desktop.

10 To continue, move the mouse ⊕ over **OK** and then press the left button.

■ Windows copies the necessary information to your computer.

11 To minimize all open windows so you can clearly view your desktop, move the mouse ⊕ over ⬚ and then press the left button.

Note: The appearance of your screen may change. To return your screen to its previous appearance, perform steps 1 to 3 on page 102, selecting (None) in step 3. Then perform step 6 on page 103.

■ The Active Desktop item appears on your screen.

Note: To move or remove the item, see page 220.

You can temporarily remove an Active Desktop item you no longer want to appear on your desktop. You can redisplay the item at any time.

The Channel Bar may appear when you first start Windows. You can remove or display the Channel Bar as you would any other Active Desktop item.

If you are using Windows 98 Second Edition, you may not have access to the Channel Bar.

REMOVE OR DISPLAY AN ITEM

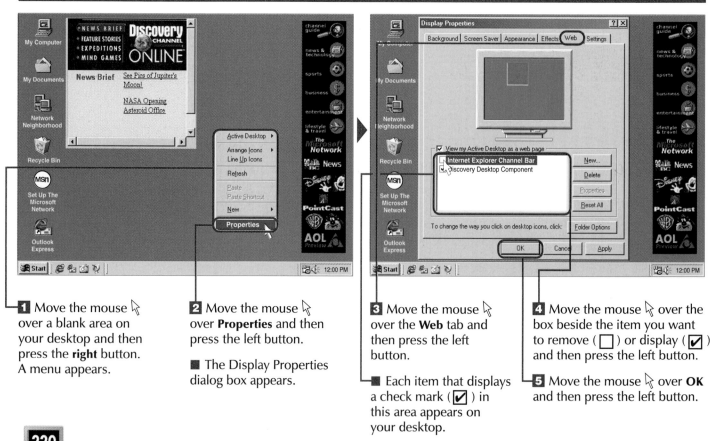

1 Move the mouse over a blank area on your desktop and then press the **right** button. A menu appears.

2 Move the mouse over **Properties** and then press the left button.

■ The Display Properties dialog box appears.

3 Move the mouse over the **Web** tab and then press the left button.

■ Each item that displays a check mark (☑) in this area appears on your desktop.

4 Move the mouse over the box beside the item you want to remove (☐) or display (☑) and then press the left button.

5 Move the mouse over **OK** and then press the left button.

You can move an Active Desktop item to a new location on your screen.

MOVE AN ITEM

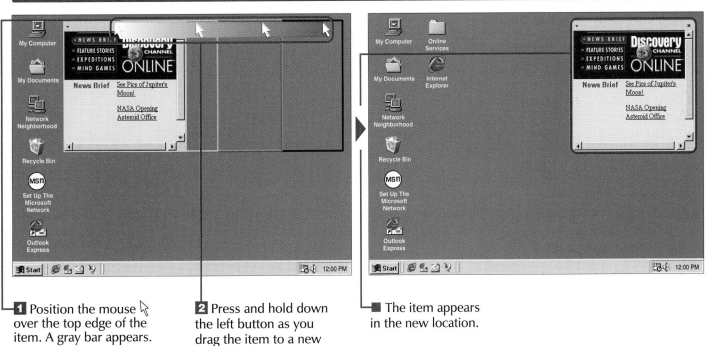

1 Position the mouse ⊳ over the top edge of the item. A gray bar appears.

2 Press and hold down the left button as you drag the item to a new location on your screen.

■ The item appears in the new location.

INDEX

OVER 6 MILLION

OTHER 3-D Visual SERIES

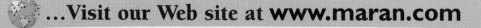

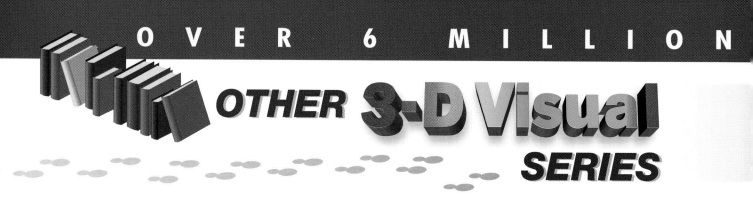

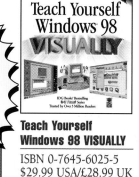
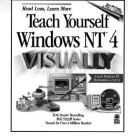

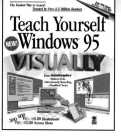
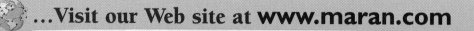

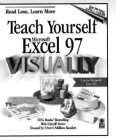

IDG BOOKS ®

TRADE & INDIVIDUAL ORDERS

Phone: **(800) 762-2974**
or **(317) 596-5200**
(8 a.m.–6 p.m., CST, weekdays)
FAX : **(800) 550-2747**
or **(317) 596-5692**

EDUCATIONAL ORDERS & DISCOUNTS

Phone: **(800) 434-2086**
(8:30 a.m.–5:00 p.m., CST, weekdays)
FAX : **(317) 596-5499**

CORPORATE ORDERS FOR 3-D VISUAL™ SERIES

Phone: **(800) 469-6616**
(8 a.m.–5 p.m., EST, weekdays)
FAX : **(905) 890-9434**

Qty	ISBN	Title	Price	Total

Shipping & Handling Charges

	Description	First book	Each add'l. book	Total
Domestic	Normal	$4.50	$1.50	$
	Two Day Air	$8.50	$2.50	$
	Overnight	$18.00	$3.00	$
International	Surface	$8.00	$8.00	$
	Airmail	$16.00	$16.00	$
	DHL Air	$17.00	$17.00	$

Subtotal _____

CA residents add
applicable sales tax _____

IN, MA and MD
residents add
5% sales tax _____

IL residents add
6.25% sales tax _____

RI residents add
7% sales tax _____

TX residents add
8.25% sales tax _____

Shipping _____

Total _____

Ship to:

Name_____

Address_____

Company_____

City/State/Zip_____

Daytime Phone_____

Payment: ☐ Check to IDG Books (US Funds Only)
☐ Visa ☐ Mastercard ☐ American Express

Card # _____ Exp. _____ Signature_____

maranGraphics™